CRAIG COOPER

GRATITUDE ON COUNTRY

A cry for a Simpler Life

D1712082

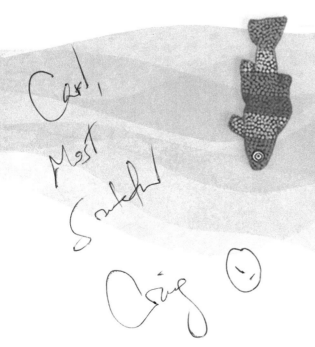

Carl,

Most

Grateful

Craig

Cooper, Craig (author)
GRATITUDE ON COUNTRY

ISBN Paperback 978-0-6454974-0-3
        E-book 978-0-6454974-1-0
WELLBEING, SELF HELP & SPIRITUALITY

Typesetting – Calluna Light 11/17
Cover Painting – Cosmic Ocean by Max Mansell

Dedication

Dedicated to my loving and devoted parents Bob and June, Surf Lifesaving Australia who taught me the appreciation of caring for people and community service, my two beautiful children Logan and Maggie, and to all First Nations people I have met on Country.

I launch this book on the 26th of May 2022, my first-born son Logan's birthday. It is also Sorry Day, an important date in the understanding of Australia's history, when we acknowledge the mistreatment of Aboriginal and Torres Strait Islander people who were forcibly removed from their families and communities, which we now know as The Stolen Generations.

Cosmic Ocean

By Max Mansell

" This painting is a gift in the spirit of Goodwill to Craig Cooper as an acknowledgement of his outstanding and selfless service to the indigenous community through Living Kaurna Culture Centre. Thank you Craig may your heart be filled with love and happiness.

A M Mansell 2011

Proceeds of this book will go towards Indigenous language programs and the concept of Gratitude on Country project (9th August Gratitude on Country).

Table of Contents

Chapter One

Born Free

I spent hours staring at the Toyota logo on the steering wheel of the 4WD, passing the miles and miles of golden red soil outside my window, as I travelled into one of the most remote locations in this great southern land. I was a young man in my early twenties, starting out on my own, free to explore what lay ahead in my life.

I was so grateful, yet perhaps did not realize how grateful I should be to come from a loving family home and community. As a young boy of four years old, I migrated to Australia with my loving parents and young brother. Leaving a large loving family behind was hard for my parents. Here I was, driving across the eastern tip of Arnhem Land in a 1988 Toyota 4WD with Surf Lifesaving logos branded across the vehicle. I was on my way to spend some time teaching children at Nhulunbuy High School and Yirrkala School about water safety, and to enjoy some Top End culture amongst the salt-water crocodiles and box jellyfish.

> ❝ Unless we are willing to encourage our children to reconnect with and appreciate the natural world, we can't expect them to help protect and care for it.
> **David Suzuki**

Family, Community, Country

Another early morning drive to swim training. Dad would walk into my bedroom, saying, "Swim training this morning, Craig?" I'd roll over the pillow and say, "Yeah, why not." I would catch up with my mates, then follow the black line up and down the pool for two hours, and enjoy some laughter at the end of the pool between the swim-sets. Some mornings my brother would join me, and Mum would take us swim training. It was hard for Dad in the mornings as he would have to get going early for his one-hour drive to work. It was a good feeling inside, having both Mum and Dad able to share the load. They also loved being part of our lives as my brother and I were growing up and I always felt grateful for that. Mum was soft and warm and Dad was funny and wise.

Surf carnivals were the best. You caught up with your mates throughout the weekend in between surf races whilst marshalling for your next event, and shared joyful humor in the surf club tent, listening to the Aussie humor and the encouragement for your club competitors as they went into the next surf event. The more years I spent on beaches across Australia competing at surf carnivals, the more the friendship and number of familiar faces grew; and to be connected to a tribe of salt warriors gave me strength to tackle other aspects of my life.

I have travelled to many beaches across this beautiful country and met some incredible people at surf clubs or surf carnivals, but when I reflect on this journey of life, it is how well I travelled that always stands out; in particular, driving across this incredible, vast country from west to east or south to north, in search of the perfect wave. The many outback towns, regional communities and soaking up the fresh air of desert, the soil and gum trees and remoteness, have always been a source of amazement at how First Nations people travelled across

Country for ceremony and trade. In the early days the car didn't have an air-conditioner, so driving with windows wide open, taking in the hot, dry fresh air along the open wide road for days, was the most liberating experience imaginable for a young soul seeking positive experiences. That has not changed to this day - the joy of driving with the window open, allowing the air to flow onto the face is such a wonderful feeling of freedom. It is the feeling that you were born free.

As English migrants arriving to Australia in 1973, Mum and Dad left a large, loving family back home. For my brother and me, the surf club at Port Noarlunga became our extended family. Life growing up with my brother always by my side was enriching and full of adventures. Russall and I grew up amongst the salty sands of Port Noarlunga (Tainburanga), an ancient spring site for a special song line and Dreaming story of the Kaurna people of Adelaide. Australia has the oldest surviving literature of songlines on Country, and as a nation we are only beginning to understand our responsibility for it.

The humor and banter my brother and I received in the surf club tent from our fellow surf club friends for how healthy the packed Esky of food was still brings a smile to my face. It took a while to understand the Australian humor. It wasn't the average lunch-box and a packet of chips. It wasn't cucumber sandwiches either. Mum and Dad valued good tucker for their boys. Fruit, nuts, juice and a range of fresh vegetables were packed for the day. My brother and I competed all day in every surf race possible at the beach, salty warriors entering the surf and competing in every possible race for our surf club, doing our club proud. Fatigue would always settle in at around 2.30 pm after an Iron Man race or board race final, and you would go for the watermelon and some dried raisins to get you through the last race of the day representing your club. It was a beautiful experience filled with wonderful memories, hard work that paid off, and laughter and warm connections on and off the beach.

Nutrition is important, as good food is what fuels the body-engine. I have added onto this belief that sometimes it is important to stop and sip on a good cup of tea and find a quiet place to reflect. I often reflect on the relationship between food and my physical fitness in those early days. When we push our body to the extreme so we may perform at our best, we occasionally stop and listen to what it needs. Watermelon, for example, was the most rewarding intake after a hard Iron Man race, fuel to replenish and restore a tired and fatigued body.

Making the most of the value of good food has been a journey for me. I have always searched for clean, whole food, noticing subtle changes in the body, recognising what foods work for individual body composition. In learning different approaches to food, I have recently enjoyed the principles of Ayurvedic, which provides insightful lessons on *doshas* and various food recipes that bring out the best in our vibration.

Dad was a dietitian in the Royal Air Force (RAF), and our meals at home were epic. There was humorous banter between Mum and Dad, and a rewarding and inspiring feast for any young boy after a day at school backed up by early morning swim training and intense surf sessions at the beach in the afternoons. Dad and Mum grew up in England during World War Two within large families, and food was limited. They had a real sense of being resourceful in the kitchen, working always with what was available in each season.

Dad famously whipped up the most amazing stews, using kidneys, liver and other meats. Today we see some of these considered waste and throw them out or use them for other purposes. I witnessed the same attention to using all the harvested food in indigenous communities, and took an interest in bush foods, (native foods). I have vivid memories of eating my first kangaroo tail around a camp fire when attending my first Garma Festival in remote Arnhem Land. Uncle

Paul Dixon, my spirit brother who passed away some years ago, introduced me to the richness of our native plants and bush foods. The 'supermarket tree' at Warriparinga was Paul's iconic story, and thousands of school children across Adelaide would visit him to listen and learn about Kaurna and Aboriginal culture.

My father and Uncle Paul passed away within 12 months of each other. I remember an event when my father was close to passing. My parents were devoted parents like most of their generation. Dad was always interested in my brother and me, and our lives, work and the many interests and hobbies that we pursued. I would visit Dad most nights and he would be would be watching TV in his bed, and one night he was watching NITV on SBS. Dad said, 'I think we chose your name well. Deadly Craig with a big smile!' Dad was open and lovingly curious about my adventures and interests in Aboriginal culture. Mum and Dad would always strive with love to keep up with my brother and me and the lives we were living.

My father always inspired me in the kitchen. His was devoted to serving up good, wholesome food, and in the early days we embraced the richness of Thai, Indian, Vietnamese, and his famous stews based on home-made stock and whatever was in season. How we have evolved from meat and three veg! Now it is protein bowls, shakes, vegan burgers and acacia food bowls in Australia, the multi-cultural society. Wholefoods, fresh organic vegetables, heirloom varieties and what's in season is becoming more on trend as we realize their overall benefits. It doesn't become more apparent than this: simply eating well - more so, encouraging children to embrace good food choices. As parents who grew up post-war, Dad and Mum had to be resourceful with food, as did most families. Dad had a good understanding of whole foods and cooking from scratch and Mum complemented him in the kitchen, so my brother and I experienced the value of home cooking and family time together at the dinner table.

Another time I travelled up to Yolgnu country, a First Nations sovereign country located on the eastern tip of northern Australia, 10 hours' drive from Darwin, the capital city of the Northern Territory. At the time I was employed by the City of Marion Council to manage the Living Kaurna Culture Centre. The Council funded myself and Jamie Goldsmith, our Cultural Education Officer, to attend the annual Garma Festival, where we observed families sitting around fires and taking part in a range of beautiful ceremonies, dance and celebration of life on country. A defining moment was when Jamie and I took part in a large group of men singing up the Country ceremony with a song-man playing the didgeridoo, more correctly named the *yidaki*. The experience is etched in my memory as a moment of love, where culture and people were devoted to caring for Country. Singing 'into' the land is a beautiful way to be grateful for country.

The intention of this ceremony is a collective value that we need all our communities to embrace: to connect to Country so we may care for it, and to remind us that we don't own Country, but Country owns us. There is much more to say on this concept of caring for Country and custodianship of Country. Songlines on land are not totems, but vibrational understanding of how Country works. Australia has the oldest literature of how land is interpreted on planet Earth, and through it we gain understanding for how energy moves across land. We then begin to see how grateful we should be for our home, that breathes for us. Singing up the land by Aboriginal men is an act of love, devotion and gratitude to Country. Songlines are not totems, but they explain and maintain the ecology of country, the lay of the land and movement of energy. Every part of the land, sea, sky and totem is part of the song-line. How grateful we should be, that our mother Earth provides us with all we need.

In the same way, my mother's love was endless. She was a good listener with warm heart and a joyful spirit. During my early years we would talk in the family room for hours. Mum's love was beautiful. Mum loved her totem, a butterfly, always growing with love into the wellbeing of our family. She gave so much warmth to my brother and me. Equally, there was no favourite; although my brother would often argue that he was the favourite son, it was not at all so. Mum valued a shared home.

My parents endured the War years in Britain, which shaped a sense of resilience in our family. We grew up with the attitude that we will always be okay and we learned to have a strong working ethic. Mum was shy in nature but once you took the time to sit with her, her warmth was endless. She was a full of light. She had a beautiful sense of humor and the ability to understand people. Mum and Dad were in love, and it is wonderful to reflect on growing up in a house that was happy. As much as they had their moments, as in any relationship, they would always work it out.

Physical Movement and Salty Life

From the early age of seven, together with my brother I spent most of my growing years at Port Noarlunga Beach. It wasn't until my later as a young adult life that I discovered how special Port Noarlunga is, and how place shapes us. Places shape our soul and our living spaces influence who we become. Tainaburang (Port Noarlunga, turning place) is part of the Tjilbruke Dreaming story. The Kaurna people of the Adelaide plains have played an important role in my understanding of Australia, and through that I hold deep respect for this ancient land and its stories and song on Country.

Surf lifesaving has been my grounding space throughout my life. It nurtured a holistic view of the world, and I saw the values of service, wellness and public safety. I have continued to understand that service is an intrinsic value. When we serve, it allows us to grow and be part of something bigger than us, thus fulfilling our own lives. Saltwater swimming has been very healing for me. It cleanses the energy around the body. There is so much evidence around the benefits of swimming in our salty oceans, and how it helps me to sustain other aspects of my life. This started in my school years, when I was challenged with volumes of study, getting enough sleep, training twice a day - up at 5 am for swim pool training and after school down to the surf club, sometimes two sessions in the afternoon, then home for jobs, school work, good food and loving parents.

High performance and deep rest are two things I have perfected over the years, although I have found, like many dads and blokes, that resting on the couch watching TV isn't the ideal environment to truly rest the body and mind! This has been an insightful learning from my early days. Understanding how we can better rest for improved performance is vitally important in order to be present and get the best out of life and the people that matter most. Sitting on the couch with a beer and watching television isn't an ideal habit for our recovery and rest period.

Like many Australian parents, Mum and Dad were devoted to their children. At Port Noarlunga and on the southern coastline of Adelaide, I would spend my time enjoying the ocean, running and hiking in the parks and scrub, and exploring the beautiful natural environment. My brother and I did our first camp in the Onkaparinga River National Park in our mid-teens, when Mum let us loose for the first time, and we camped overnight in the Onkaparinga Gorge. As a young teenager, being free to explore nature gave me a sense of wonderment. We explored the coastline, scrub and tracks and I gained a sense of confidence that built trust in my outer and inner world. It is more challenging today for some young people to have this opportunity, as we see more of our environment becoming urbanised.

We seem to be building more and more concrete environments and homes surrounded by more homes and built environment. This is particularly the case for communities and families that live in big cities. Local governments are endeavoring to green our cities, which provides some hope and inspiration for how we may live on country better. We are part of nature; we need green for our wellbeing.

Moving Out of Home

My first trip to the Northern Territory was when I secured full-time employment after completing a Diploma from TAFE and a Bachelor's Degree in Business from University of South Australia. I left Adelaide (Kaurna country) in July 1990. I secured a job as a Lifesaving Development Officer for Surf Lifesaving Australia. This was the third time I'd left Adelaide for an extended period of time.

After Year 12, I had ventured off overseas to Europe, backpacking and exploring villages and seeking my heritage and family, which had been foreign to me. When returning to Australia, as part of my study I moved up to the Gold Coast with my brother and a fellow surf lifesaver, Simon Martin. At the time, Kellogg's Nutri-Grain Iron Man racing was strongly featured across the news and Australian television. Living on the Gold Coast enabled me to take my sport to the next level. I returned home that year and at 19 years of age I won the Open Board Title as a first-year senior competitor against the legends of Board Paddling and Surf Lifesavers I had admired as a young fella - Gavin Hill, a legend of Australian Board Paddling, and Dwayne Thuys a World Iron Man Champion.

I repeated the win two years later, but by then I was immersed in and curious to understand the rich culture of Aboriginal ceremony. I was only just beginning to understand parts of culture, lore, moiety and song on Country. Initially when working for Surf Lifesaving Australia in Darwin, I travelled and experienced parts of Gove Peninsular and Nhunlunbuy and Yirrikala always respectfully listening to Country and people across the Top End.

A defining experience will always be my regular drive across Arnhem Land on the Gove Track. I will always remember the smell of country being burnt by fire management and First Nation rangers, and the sight of red soils and stringy-bark vegetation whilst listening to the stillness of Country. This experience still sits inside me today; I experienced how Country can move your soul and give you a sense of appreciation of its sacredness.

Australia was not natural in 1788, but made. It was not land or dirt, as some would see the natural world, but 'Country', an English word that Aboriginal people have transformed. Country is physical, communal and spiritual, and encompasses water, sky, habitats, sites, places, totems and relationships; it is a world of the mind, a way of believing and behaving. Creator ancestors made Country in the Dreaming, and they still oversee Country, sacred Country.

The Gove Track, as it is called, goes from Katherine in the Northern Territory to Barunga, crossing the river at Beswick, and Bulman, and the final stretch to East Arnhem. The track less travelled, it always gave a sense of adventure with the red soils, vegetation and burn-off. It is all unsealed road, and in the wet season the Yolgnu people are cut off from the rest of the world, as the track is inaccessible. I will always be grateful to have crossed Country as sacred as this.

In January 1911, the Northern Territory separated from South Australia and transferred its governance role as its own government territory and administration. I met many South Australians calling Darwin home and there were plenty of jokes and humour about South Australia wanting the Northern Territory to come back and join the

State of South Australia again. In 1990 the Northern Territory had two surf clubs, Darwin and Gove.

As a young fella, leaving my brother and folks back in Port Noarlunga to go and live in Darwin was hard at first. It was such a long way from home. But on only my third day in Darwin, I somehow ended up on a 21-seater bus on the way to Broome Surf Club in Western Australia, for the Pearl Classic Surf Carnival Festival. We stopped along the way at Kununurra and Fitzroy Crossing. It was quite an initiation to Top End culture and First Nations people in far north-west communities. As a young, fit fella from down south, I competed in the surf carnival and won the Open Board, Ski, Swim and Iron Man. The medals were beautifully made locally from pearl shells, and the hospitality of the Broome Surf Club community was warm and welcoming. After two days in Broome, the 21-seater bus returned to Darwin. It was an 1890-km one-way trip, 4,000 kms return, a long road trip for a two-day surf carnival!

The friendship between Broome, Darwin and Gove Surf Clubs was incredible considering the distance between the three surf clubs across the Top End of Australia. They had a common connection of community service and love of the salty ocean. The road trip was entertaining with the Darwin Surf Club President elected for the following year of, Creeky (Bob), who was an epic harmonica player and kept the bus in good spirits during the long drive to Broome. The experience had a feeling of what it would have been in the early days of Australians exploring Country and seeking meaning of Country. Being on the bus for this trip with surf lifesavers was an adventure of a lifetime.

Salt Water Healing and Road Trips

Travelling across country as a surf lifesaver was something many club-bies did during the '70s, '80s and '90s, when Australian Surf Lifesaving Championships were held in different states across Australia. Surf lifesavers from all parts of Australia would travel across the country to meet once a year for the Australian Surf Lifesaving Championships. It was the ultimate road trip, with surf craft, big surf boats, and equipment surf trailers in tow. It was a great way to see Australia with surf clubbies friends. I didn't realise at the time that I was feeling the country and listening and connecting to the land, from Anglesea, Wollongong, Moana, Perth, Maroochydore, Burleigh Heads, Torquay, Collaroy, to Kurrawa and Scarborough, Western Australia.

Those early days travelling in a car was on equal terms with flying. The cost of airfares was slightly higher and a luxury for some. To fill a car with surf friends was a wonderful team-building and bonding experience, a good way to build relationships with friends for life on your way to an interstate or regional surf carnival. When it is done well with adult leadership and supervision, male bonding allows for shared experiences and wisdom to come forth. Sharing a long drive with surf mates and checking that all is okay and firmly strapped and secure on the gear trailer across the Hay Plains of New South Wales was a beautiful contrast to surf skis and malibus and aquatic lifesaving equipment amongst the dusty outback of vast Australia.

This epic adventure occurred every year over a number of decades. Grumpy old men in surf clubs would talk about Bancoora, Victoria, Surf Titles of 1977 and the size of the waves and surf boat wipe-outs. As a young person, I found my thirst for waves across country was never far from my mind. To have bragging rights about Top End surfing amongst crocodiles and box jellyfish on the eastern tip of Arnhem Land is the ultimate surf adventure. Turtle Beach is a remote coastal destination that Gove Peninsula patrol on the odd occasion. With a nice little wave rolling in, it gives you the feeling you have landed in paradise, and with a constant crocodile spotter you feel slightly okay to relax into the coastal cove of tropical splendor.

On my second trip to Arnhem Land, I met Stuart Kellaway, bass guitar for the band 'Yothu Yindi'. Stuart was a keen surfer and also the music teacher at Yirrkala Community School. As a young surf salt person, I found it very exciting to meet Stuart. At this time the song Treaty was an international hit song. Treaty was released by Tribal Voice in June 1991, and was the first Aboriginal song to attain international recognition, peaking at number 6 on the Billboard Dance Club play charts.

Then, in October 1992, the Treaty was performed by Yothi Yindi in New York, United States of America, at the launch of the United Nations International Year for the World's Indigenous Peoples.

The United Nations Declaration on the Rights of Indigenous Peoples (UNDRIP) was first adopted by the General Assembly on Thursday, 13 September 2007, by a majority of 144 states in favour, 4 votes against (Australia, Canada, New Zealand and the United States) and 11 abstentions (Azerbaijan, Bangladesh, Bhutan, Burundi, Colombia, Georgia, Kenya, Nigeria, Russian Federation, Samoa and Ukraine).

Years later the four countries that voted against have reversed their position and now support the UN Declaration. Today the Declaration is the most comprehensive international instrument on the rights of indigenous peoples. It establishes a universal framework of minimum standards for the survival, dignity and wellbeing of the indigenous peoples of the world and it elaborates on existing human rights standards and fundamental freedoms as they apply to the specific situation of indigenous peoples.

Wikipedia

It was so inspiring to see a man teaching music to young children at the local school. Stuart had an interest in establishing a surf lifesaving club in Arnhem Land for the benefit of young people; it would be the first indigenous surf club in Australia. It wasn't until I returned in 2010 with Kaurna Cultural Officer Jamie Goldsmith to experience the richness of Garma Cultural Festival, the largest Aboriginal Festival in Australia, that we reconnected to Stuart to see this dream come to fruition. Surf Lifesaving Northern Territory (SLSNT) supported the project. The surf club was established in 2009; it was named *Walngawu Djakamirri* meaning 'Carer of Life' in Yolnu Matha, the language of north-east Arnhem Land. I visited again as a volunteer for SLSNT the following year when undertaking further water safety programs for the Yolgnu school children.

The Saltwater people of East Arnhem land hold a special place in my heart. With custodianship across land and the beauty of a rich sea culture, the Yolgnu people and their art, story and language connect land and sea as one. As an ocean lover who is always grateful for the healing experiences of saltwater nurturing my soul, I deeply respect the interwoven messages that allow me to see 'self' more clearly on this journey of life. I fell in love with this culture, and during those early years found myself being lost in Yolgnu and Kaurna culture. The Kaurna people also so deservedly call themselves Saltwater people. This ground's my soul and I am able to connect as best I can, as a white fella that deeply respects this ancient land that has been cared for since the beginning of time.

Surfing and catching a Malibu wave has always given me the flow to reconnect to myself, cleanse my space and re-energise the vigor, zest for life and big-hearted adventurous man that I am. Taking this journey of discovering who we are is the most important journey we all need to take. We are always evolving and becoming someone who is uniquely our self.

I remember a time when I was travelling five hours west of Alice Springs, and saw an unusual sight, a young fella from Western Australia with a dog and five camels. I stopped my 4WD and we spoke at length. The young man from Western Australia had been travelling for two years throughout central Northern Territory, Queensland and Western Australia. He didn't know much about camels at the beginning of his trek. We shared the concept of who we are becoming as a daily joy, in which we are always evolving and witnessing our growth. Spending time with a dog, five camels and enough supplies to last 12 days provides the space and solitude for a man to find himself and witness those changes and personal growth. We shared the beauty of seeing the early morning star across the outback morning horizon; I have only shared this morning star story with one another person. Today I share with you all the love of the morning star.

> " Barnumbirr, also known as Banumbirr or Morning Star, is a creator-spirit in the Yolngu culture of Arnhem Land in the Northern Territory of Australia, who is identified as the planet Venus. In Yolngu Dreaming mythology, she is believed to have guided the first humans, the Djanggawul sisters, to Australia. After the Djanggawul sisters arrived safely near Yirrkala (at Yalangbara) in North East Arnhem Land, Barnumbirr flew across the land from east to west, creating a songline which named and created the animals, plants and geographical features.
> **From DBPedia**

As I sat on the sand at surf carnivals with a towel over my head, marshalling for surf races, the art of Zen and being present evolved for me. I spent 30-plus years competing at surf carnivals, in the marshalling area, and lining up to race and perform, always taking the time to rest the heart rate, preparing the mind to race and be relaxed. As a fair-skinned bloke conscious of the rays of sunshine, I was mindful to ensure that I was hydrated and feeling balanced and that my mind was focused on being strong and ready to race. Visualizing the moments of my race, I would plan a blend of meditation technique; being relaxed was vitally important in approaching any surf swim race, Iron Man or board final.

My most memorable race was when I won the gold medal in the Masters Ocean Malibu Race at the 2012 World Lifesaving Championship, with my brother finishing in second place. I had lost my father the year before and was struggling with some aspects of my life. I dedicated the race to my father, for being a stable figure in my life and for leaving England with Mum for a better life for my brother and me. Dad was always there for us. We knew how much pain he endured in parts of his life due to ill-health, yet he kept getting up and going on with a beautiful sense of humor that would make Mum smile.

Sometimes in life we can love something so much that we become lost, and later realize that have other parts of our life which are just as important are out of balance. I felt I had a rescue mission, as a devoted lifesaver, perhaps to rescue or to understand how we can resuscitate and pay true respect the oldest surviving culture on planet earth, acknowledging what western culture has done to it. But it has survived.

We move forward in life to explore other aspects that will enrich our character and take us to serving in other ways, yet still honouring the roots established in a Sunday surf patrol between the flags. My good friend Di Wallace Ward was the first women to win the World Iron Woman race in the late 1990s. She was a wonderful ambassador for women in surf lifesaving, and she planted a healthy perspective on life. In a casual conversation, Di urged me, 'Do what you can stay true to your roots.' From this I went on to discover coaching, having always been interested in personal development.

Journeying with my brother in the saltwater space has been wonderful, fun and full of beautiful memories, with our common bond, love, and shared parts of our lives. We have ventured away from each other with our own families and work, but we have always come back together on the saltwater. This is so common in surf-land, with siblings in shared pursuits and extended family connections.

The grounding energy of salt on my skin has deeply penetrated into my soul. The thousands of hours of swimming, surfing and paddling along the coastline does something to a man. It cleans the soul so he sees things clearly, and enables the 'giving game' of life. When we are blessed with seeing our self-worth, we dare to take the journey less travelled. I am grateful to have experienced some wonderful moments as a man. I feel I have truly lived. But I don't consider myself any different to any other bloke with his own unique experiences. As I continue to serve in the business, wellness and coaching space, I constantly see that we all have magical stories inside us. There is nothing more rewarding than to have empowered the many clients that I have served to extract their own unique, wonderful stories.

Family - Children and Fatherhood

In February 1994 I married Kym, a farmer's daughter and a beautiful lady. We met at the local swimming centre where we were both teaching swimming to school-age children. After we married, I supported Kym whilst she studied to become a primary school teacher. It was an enriching experience to see her become a wonderful teacher. I loved every moment being an active, supportive and loving father to the two most precious people in my life, our children. It is a gift to see your children grow up becoming wonderful young adults.

My son Logan was born on 26 May, 1996 (26 May is also Sorry Day, a special day in the story of Aboriginal Australia and the beginning of Reconciliation Week), and Maggie was born on 28 March, 1999. Both my children followed their own paths and dreams in the performing arts, Maggie in dance, choir and drama, running her own business, and Logan in music production after graduating with a Bachelor of Music (Sonic Arts) from Adelaide University. Kym and I ended our marriage amicably in 2013, having experienced the joy of nurturing two beautiful children.

Families can be stressful with the competing needs of the focus on the wellbeing of your children and finding intimacy in the relationship, which can be challenging in any relationship. In terms of relationships, what coaching allows us to do is take the dive into personal development and acquire the skills to navigate and understand the concept of self-care, self-love, ensuring that our feelings and emotions are clearly intact on the journey to discovering our own self.

Most people would know me as a kind, gentle man with a big heart. My insightful lesson in life is the importance of having strong boundaries and being okay to say no whilst also recognising I have reached my capacity. However, I have found that sometimes when you lose self in an ancient culture it becomes a long journey to return, without turning your back on what you have learnt, and to share the learned wisdom for the greater good. I see myself as a high achiever and I have always been striving for a better society, caring for people deeply. People change for the better if we seek growth with an open mind, but the essence of self is still the same. It has been quite a ride to return to a stronger and wiser self, but I will not stop serving for a better community and I will ensure I love the people that matter most in my life.

Coaching has provided some wonderful concepts and frameworks which have allowed my business to serve in this space, and empower and reach more people while still honouring my own personal life. Our children remind us to think ahead. What we want to pass onto them that is important: wisdom, love and an optimistic outlook on life. We want for them a future that looks hopeful, fair and equitable, where love filters through across community and Country.

Within my family structure, I took on the role of hero-warrior and provider, and the concept of self-care and being able to hold equanimity while remaining calm in a stressful situation took on a new meaning. I began to discover what is really going on in the world. In losing my father, and also attending Aboriginal funerals regularly, I began to understand the impact of complex trauma on people's lives.

My time connecting to Country and First Nations culture reminds me that our system needs to treasure these values, the sacredness of children, and a culture that nurtures wholeness through our experiences and an inter-generational approach in sharing our wisdom with our children. Community wisdom and the success of a society is achieved when we value our elders and their ongoing contribution to the circle of life. When Uncle Steve Goldsmith was filming at Warriparinga for Postcards, a Channel 9 TV show featuring Living Kaurna Culture Centre, my two children were fortunate to appear with him on a tour of the wetland where he talked about how to find food in the bush.

I have seen many First Nations people sacrifice and endure their story, knowing they wouldn't be around to see change. This is the core of the concept of planting trees for shade for future generations. An old friend who passed away a few years ago, an Aboriginal man who loved sharing his knowledge of Aboriginal art, devoted his life to teaching refugees and migrants symbols, patterns and stories on canvas; it was a powerful symbol of love towards people coming onto this ancient country, with the aim of creating respect for Aboriginal culture that isn't always received from the broader community. Things are changing because people who are not devoted to public recognition have worked at grass roots level to bring this about. I write this book for those early adopters who saw the wisdom to build a collective, shared vision for Australia whilst sharing the ancient wisdom with those who showed interest and respect for song, art, culture and dreaming. Let us not forget the unsung silent community cultural leaders who have passed away far too young while fighting for the culture of Country that could have so easily been forgotten.

For many decades, Australia did not respect this ancient culture, but was fearful of what was foreign to their own culture on the other side of planet. In a clash of cultures, so we labelled it savage, and classified Aboriginal people as part of Australia's flora and fauna under our legislation. This book isn't about the horrendous crimes and genocide that have occurred on this land. My heart hurts when I reflect on the people I have seen and the shock of communities still struggling today to navigate the western world. There has been trauma and a culture has been decimated, yes, but in the new story, the Australian Aborigine has survived. Some First Nations people have walked between the two worlds and achieved wonderful things for their people, for all of us to enjoy, but for many the long road is still ahead. To those who fought so hard, advocating with anger at what was considered right for a beautiful, enriching culture, I say this: your words have not been wasted and your life of fighting for your culture has contributed to my story and other people's stories, and we will not forget what has been endured.

I evolved into a man who loves black culture, the wisdom that First Nations culture teaches us about caring for Country, a civilized culture whose people understood their role in the universe and how-to live-in harmony. Theirs was a simple but beautiful life. I was caught up with the politics of the struggle of Aboriginal culture, the fight to be recognised in mainstream Australia. I witnessed racism at first hand with the many Aboriginal people I met and engaged with. I was often upset at seeing good Aboriginal people being unfairly treated in our modern society. My father lived inside me, the man who would always support the underdog in our football league. As a young boy, I would ask Dad, who do you support? Dad would always respond, The team at the bottom of the ladder. In seeking the meaning of an 'underdog', I was curious to understand why the minority or a particular social issue isn't treated fairly and how it can breed inequality within our society.

I recall one time in my early twenties when I was at Tennant Creek in the Northern Territory. An Aboriginal man was standing on the side of the road, and he was frightened to cross the road. He had been drinking alcohol. He looked at me with a smile and signaled if I could assist him across the road. I walked across the road to help him and we crossed the road together so he could be with his family in the park under the shade of trees. The man was extremely grateful. I later learnt there had been many accidents on roads in the Territory, where trucks had hit inebriated Aboriginal people. It is small gestures that build trust and kindness.

During Reconciliation Week in May, 2009, Uncle Steve, his son Jamie and Uncle Paul were yarning on the front deck at Warriparinga Culture Centre. Steve was talking about how Yolgnu culture played an important part in bringing back song and dance onto Kaurna land with cultural brother Karl Telfer and others. We wanted to find a project to bring awareness of the Saltwater people of Adelaide. Paul provided some beautiful insights into what the Adelaide plains were like before white fellas arrived. Wetlands extended through most of the Adelaide city area. There was good fishing and country. The magpie geese could be seen far across the plains, and plenty of freshwater was holding the abundance of country. From Warriparinga Culture Centre, the walk to the top of hill today takes you to Flinders Medical Centre and Flinders University, from where you would see all of your Country across Adelaide. You also could see Narunga people (York Peninsula, South Australia) travelling onto Kaurna Country, with smoke from the fires, and magpie geese startling the Country as they travelled.

There was talk and yarning about canoes being a good mode of transport across country and how good it would be to make a traditional canoe from a River Red Gum. Two hours in, we were discussing how we could make the canoe project happen, when the wind blew in and Uncle Moogy Sumner, Ngarendjeri elder, walked into the culture Centre with a smile.

We had to comply with Council's risk procedures to ensure the canoe would be made safely. We embraced modern technology through Kennard's hire, with a cherry picker lifting device, whilst still researching what tools were required to cut the bark out of the tree successfully according to the old ways. The making of the canoe was the platform for engaging with other Aboriginal men. Paul's brother Adam and other men heard the news. We consulted with Dr Neal Draper, an archaeologist, whose business kindly supported the project, and with his expertise we walked across Country to find the right tree. 48 hours later, ABC Behind the News, Channel 7 and ABC Radio had contacted Warriparinga Culture Centre. The project featured on ABC Behind the News, teaching children about Aboriginal culture and canoe making. The canoe featured at the 2009 Reconciliation week. Today it hangs in the Living Kaurna Culture Centre gallery.

Uncle Paul Dixon's passing was a significant event for Warriparinga. As a white fella taking part in a sacred event, I found it a humbling experience. A fire was made the old way and we kept it burning for several days until Paul had passed away. Many people visited the fire. Young Paul, his son, came to the fire, and many others to pay their respects. A special moment was when we took some of the fire and smoke into Flinders Medical Centre in Karl Telfers Coolamon. I called Flinders Hospital to explain and asked if we could visit Paul. A few hours later they called me back and allowed us to take the smoke into the hospital, advising that we had 45 minutes to take the fire ceremony into Paul's room. Flinders Medical Centre turned the smoke alarms off, which was a beautiful gesture in which we see western culture adapting to accommodate the ancient protocols of First Nation wisdom.

Ten men, including Dr Rob Amery (Adelaide University School of Indigenous Languages) and myself, walked up the hill from Warriparinga, into Flinders Medical Centre, to honour Paul Dixon, his role and his life. In the early days when the land was subject to a potential housing development, Kaurna community wanted to ensure the land was not developed because of its cultural significance as a lore ground and gateway to the Tjilbruke Dreaming story and the peace lore on Country. As in the story of Vincent Lingiari and Paul Kelly's song *From Little Things Big Things Grow,* Paul had squatted and 'sat on Country' when he moved into an old homestead (Fairford House) as the custodian of Warriparinga.

After Uncle Paul Dixon's passing, Paul was made a life member of the South Australian Native Food Association for his contribution to hosting many bush food forums and workshops across the Adelaide metropolitan region. At the funeral, the family asked me to be his spirit brother and hold onto the spirit of Warriparinga and when his son (Paul Junior) was old enough, to share Paul's spirit and Warriparinga with Paul Junior. Paul Junior and myself have been catching up during the writing of this book, as we travel across Country allowing his son to connect to Country.

It has been a heavy burden, yet humbling, to realise my role and who I have become through these events. I have gained a much deeper meaning and a sense of appreciation of Country and how we can be connected to a special place.

In April 2011, after a few days away in central Australia, I drew a map of Australia. While sitting on Country, this narrative map was an impression of my story as it was unfolding. For many years, my mantra for Country has been *Salt Water Healing, Desert Dreaming*, and it featured strongly on my narrative therapy map. I titled the map 'For the love of our children and our future children'. Perhaps it is a metaphor to describe my own journey and chunking up into big picture dreaming. My hope is that all Australians can connect with a collective vision so we may appreciate what's important in life, that we may focus on passing our culture to the next generation, and that the wellbeing of our children is always at the forefront of our minds.

The Passing of Uncle David

David Dalaithngu (known as David Gulpilil) was an accomplished actor, dancer and painter. Many celebrated roles in Australian films, such as *Rabbit Proof Fence*, *Storm Boy*, *Crocodile Dundee*, *Walkabout*, *Charlie's Country* and *The Tracker*, saw him gain a reputation as one of the country's greatest actors. His passing was timely. I truly believe souls who inspire the collective and greater good choose their passing for the betterment of collective consciousness. Safe travels wherever you may travel.

On 1 December 2021, during the passing of David Dalaithngu, I was in the final stages of writing my book, and residing in Middleton, not far from where David was residing in Murray Bridge. I always look for signs that it is time to move forward into a space that will test my character, and this was clearly a moment to move forward a pledge to Australia to acknowledge our First Nations people for caring for Country for thousands and thousands of years. David Dalaithngu had played the role of a Yolngu man in *Storm Boy*, my favorite film when I was a young boy. I was fascinated by spirit and the pelican, how it gracefully flew into the sea and the wetlands for all to see. We always take meaning when events occur in our life, events that come from our environment. Today I chose to honour the little boy inside me.

Children's Dreaming Totems and Custodianship

If we are to awaken to a new Australia and ensure our culture sustains itself within our environment, we must begin with our children. First Nations people have cared for Country for thousands and thousands of years. One of the components woven through the ancient culture is giving children a totem or a few totems, so they begin to connect with and understand Country and how it interacts with our environment. Schools and communities could engage with First Nation elders on this idea. Conservation biologist Professor Stephen Hopper, from the University of Western Australia, has been engaging with Elders with regard to this concept. In adopting a totem, you become associated with an animal and/or a plant; they become you and you become them.

The concept is very powerful and effective, and a simple idea. Taking this approach must be followed with respect while forming respectful relationships with community Elders. If we are to start seeing an Australia where we begin to walk the two paths, our children can play a sustaining part in the way forward for generations to come. Totems connect people on a spiritual level, providing deeper connectivity, an understanding of their clan group, their traditional land and dreaming. Depending on where a person is from, they could have three or more totems which represent their nation or clan. Family totems are predetermined, but personal totems are appointed. My own totem came from walking on Country, being respectfully curious, and demonstrating a caring interest in aspects of country.

Teachers and schools would be advised to make connection with Elders and community members of the Country on which they are working, to invite them into to talk about totems. This way, meaningful dialogue about history, connection to Country and obligation are taught by the first teachers of this nation. We could see every Australian child being given a plant and animal totem when they start preschool. Every immigrant could be given a totem plant and animal when they are naturalised. This would be a respectful pathway to a sense of appreciation and gratitude for our beautiful country.

Custodianship or stewardship is a value-imposed philosophy of understanding how we live and care for our home. When you have a totem you see the world differently, you see your connection more clearly, and you respect environment more deeply. Yes, we are all custodians, but this system of totems and custodianship isn't taken lightly. It requires us to follow protocols and a lifestyle. It is earned and it comes with obligations. I feel it would be a worthy conversation to have across communities and schools, and respectful dialogue with Aboriginal Elders would enable other Australians to being to understand and walk together as one.

Australia could lead the world by example. **Let us act our real age.** I believe we need to see clearly that the best way forward for our country's biggest problem, is within our First Nations' culture. How we embrace our national identity will make us stronger both as individuals and a collective. Genocide of the oldest surviving culture on planet earth took place in Australia. Indigenous people across the world have been conquered and decimated and it has never been right. It is part of our story, and if we don't own our mistakes and embrace our truth, how can we move forward into trust, love and harmony and grow as one? Let us act our age. We are a very old country and we should lead the world by our example. It is not enough to choose not to take part in any political party or past government policy that hasn't worked. This issue is too important to take sides or bicker, as we often see and hear on television and radio.

Indigenous people didn't argue within their culture. On the 14 February, Uncle Lewis O'Brien (92 year old Kaurna Senior Elder) shared with me that the culture had 'reached a level of sophistication that lore was clearly defined'. There was no need to argue or debate, leading to political divide. The culture learned to lean into what serves us: to collaborate and together find the best way forward on matters that arose. The essence of coaching and good leadership is to lean into trust and what is best for people and place. Is this not true?

On 9 August each year, the United Nations' (UN) International Day of the World's Indigenous Peoples recognises the role Indigenous people across the world in contributing to custodianship and caring for Country. I make a pledge in the final chapter of this book that we lean into this, draw a line the sand, and set a new tone and write a new story for all Australians to embrace and participate in. This isn't about the Australia Day argument or a political debate; it is leaning into what is good and true about what matters most in life - the wellbeing of people and place for future generations. We need to understand that certain things aren't working, we need to own our mistakes, learn, and feel okay about taking this journey, for us to realise what is at the core of us.

Trust is at the core of all relationships and First Nations people have every right to tread with caution. Trust has been broken and promises have not been delivered. We have seen lies from our political system, and deception does not serve the common good. Business and good trade on Country values trust and accountability. I see many families with small to medium size (SME) businesses working hard to make ends meet. The core of our country is built on lies and does not embrace truth. When truth and trust are embraced across all aspects of life, especially in business and relationships, we begin to see what we can truly achieve: outcomes that transform people and place.

Yoga, Meditation, Coaching and My Journey of Healing

My journey has been one of healing. Wellness is healing, and we are healing all the time, finding the strength to move forward towards wholeness without letting go of an important story that needs to be nurtured. I have found Aboriginal people are deeply spiritual; as individuals they understand who they are and embrace spirituality in their lives. That allows us to be stronger and have a sense of what's important to us. I believe spirit should be embraced by everyone. Spirit isn't religion, but a concept of connecting to our higher self and to divine source.

After my departure from the Living Kaurna Culture Centre, I was most fortunate to find Shakti Durga and her Yoga Ashram on the east coast of Australia, south of Newcastle, New South Wales. I discovered yoga and kirtan, I read books on Bhakti yoga, and I began to engage in a regular meditation practice.

The growth of yoga and meditation and communities embracing emotional wellbeing is a wonderful sign that we are moving into more wholeness and wellness on Country, through modern yoga, traditional yoga and the ways in which other cultural groups across Australia hold onto their ceremony and rituals. First Nations people, like Uncle Steve Goldsmith, would say they have always welcomed different cultures around the fire. Culture does shape and change, so it serves what is good for people and place.

United Nations Declaration of Human Rights

10 December 2021

Leading into the weekend of the two-year anniversary of my mother passing away on 13 December 2019, the 2021 United Nations Human Rights Day theme was 'equality'. The theme was taken from Article 1 of the Declaration, which says that all human beings are born free and equal in dignity and rights.

At the celebration of my mother's life, we played one of her favourite songs, *Born Free*. When we look at the concept of being born free, we see that every day when we wake up and see the sun rise, we have the opportunity to be born again. We can let go of our mistakes, embrace the wisdom from the previous day and be born again to move forward with greater clarity and lean into what is good for us. The 'inner child' is a beautiful coaching meditation technique that we use to nurture our true self. We are each born perfect. When our mothers bring us into this world, we have all the resources to be whole and full of love and enjoy life. Our Mother Earth provides all we need. Let us use these resources wisely for everyone to enjoy.

Today I stand in my truth and recognise the oldest surviving culture on planet earth, the culture of our first Australians. I have experienced the struggle between both worlds in small ways myself. I have fallen down many times in this life and the journey has cost me and my family much, but today I am owning it. I did not experience the genocide path that my Indigenous brothers and sisters have experienced and continue to experience. But I have listened well to the narrative for a long time and thought about how best to respond and provide a bridge or platform where Australia can truly recognise respectfully the concept of cultivating wellness back onto Country. I am no different to anyone else, and my story is standing in my truth.

The Universal Declaration of Human Rights is a milestone document, which proclaims the inalienable rights that everyone is entitled to as a human being, regardless of race, colour, religion, sex, language, political or other opinion, national or social origin, property, birth or other status.

> **"** Where, after all, do universal human rights begin? In small places, close to home – so close and so small that they cannot be seen on any maps of the world. Unless these rights have meaning there, they have little meaning anywhere. Without concerted citizen action to uphold them close to home, we shall look in vain for progress in the larger world.
> **Eleanor Roosevelt**

To share a vision and a common value for a better world is a good thing for everyone to strive towards. For all of us to be well - Living Well Australia - is to pause and reflect, and bring our mind to this vision, is it not? We are divided at the moment. Our collective consciousness is disturbed and impacting on people's wellbeing, particularly their emotions. Yet this is life, is it not?

9 August is recognised by the United Nations as International Day of the World's Indigenous Peoples, particularly for their contribution to environmental protection and the concept of custodianship and stewardship of Country and the Earth. Our First Nations people have the oldest surviving culture on the planet, and are the greatest farmers and the greatest dreamers. This country is built on sacred ground and sacred ceremony, yet every public holiday is a booze festival. Alcohol continues to shape a large part of our culture. Let us have a healthy perspective on this topic.

" The power of love is political, its social, it's not
a flaky idea of being romantical, don't act out of
anger don't act out of fear or out of anxiety, but act
out of love. When you act out of love your action
will have more meaning and more fulfilling and
your actions will excel and create its own intrinsic
meaning for you and everyone. If you are a political,
environmental or social activist act out of love.
**Satish Kumar, United Nations –
Peace Walk Activist**

Uncle Charlie

During my time at Warriparinga, my administration support officer
was Leonie Bray, a wonderful lady from Alice Springs. Leonie was the
niece of Charlie Perkins, an Aboriginal activist, soccer player, the first
Indigenous Australian man to graduate in tertiary education, from the
University of Sydney, and known for his instigation and organisation
of the 1965 Freedom Ride. The Freedom Ride involved student activists travelling across country NSW and highlighting Aboriginal people
were not allowed into public swimming pools. In Warriparinga, I was
managing both the Marion Swimming Centre and Living Kaurna
Culture Centre. Uncle Steve first pointed this out to me and shared
the story of Uncle Charlie and Leonie's family connection.

Aussies love nicknames, do we not! I have been called many things
- Coops, Crackles, Craigas, CC and Bloodnut. Uncle Steve and Uncle
Paul would call me 'Charlie Craig'. It is one fond memory I treasure
from the time I was travelling with Leonie Bray and Steve Goldsmith
to Canberra. We were going there to listen Kevin Rudd make his
famous speech in Parliament on 13 February, 2008, a motion of

Apology to Indigenous Australians. It was a formal apology on behalf of the successive parliaments and governments whose policies and laws 'inflicted profound grief, suffering and loss on these our fellow Australians'.

> " Believe and dream the journey has begun. Let us dream and believe the journey has only had a bump. Ancient dreamers believe in some basics - we only need to re-begin. We can make it if we stick to the basics. Believe me, it has been done for 60,000 years and more... we love what they have done. We can make it or break it. I believe love for people and Country will ensure it won't be undone. The basics of our culture are to love one another on Country. The Dreamers, the Dreamers, the great Dreamers inspire us to Dream again.
>
> **Charlie Craig, NAIDOC week, July 2011**

Chapter Two

Cultivating Consciousness in Self

66 When we begin to know ourselves in an open
and self-supportive way, we take the first step to
encourage our children to know themselves.
Daniel J. Siegel

Modern Man

To embrace our inner self is to listen to our mind and become aware of what is coming into our zone of energy. It is an interesting concept that our mind is separate from our brain. If we are subtly aware of our thoughts and how the thoughts of others impact our own self, we begin to distinguish our true self and be less influenced by others. Our tribes and the people in our lives play a role in influencing us, and these sub-cultures have an impact on the thought patterns that play out.

Sometimes we may have no awareness that people and events are having an impact on our being. A man's traditional journey has been in the doing, the task of completing jobs that our modern western world has imposed upon us. Today we are consumers of products and services. The challenge of life is to survive and thrive whilst we provide for the matriarch, 'the mother and child', yet today we see a dominant patriarch playing out within our society, and the rise of the feminine and an evolving modern work culture. A patriarchal system is governed by the man or masculine energy, and the matriarchal system is governed by the women or feminine energy.

The changing face of our modern society means that some of our men are being left behind. First Nations men in particular have had their traditional roles taken away. Their loss of identify has impacted significantly on the contribution and decimation of Aboriginal culture. Indigenous cultures across the world remained in harmony with Mother Nature by understanding both forms of governance and social structures, which meant that the matriarchal and patriarchal systems supported one another.

Uncle Lewis O'Brien, a 92-year-old Kaurna Elder. David Suzuki said that 'like an Australian Mandela, O'Brien shares his life and thoughts without rancor or bitterness'. Uncle Lewis insightfully shared a duality concept, the idea that all things in our life that sustain and bring goodness to our world come in twos. The Kaurna word that describes how we see all things in our environment as equal is *Pa*, (Bar) which equates to a 'duality concept', *'Yara'*. When we under-stand 'Concepts' we are better equipped to experience the universe more fully. Yara means – different, distinct and separate. The word *'pa'* (Bar) means everything is equal, man and woman, tree, bird, soil, ocean, kangaroo. The correlation between these two words equates to becoming more whole as we navigate ourself through the universe. Interestingly *'Yara'* by nature plays out as reciprocally (reciprocal) in that an equal exchange between two people or two living systems or a bird and a tree concept.

The mobile phone dominates our lives. Every time we hear a noise coming from our phone, it interrupts a real-life conversation in which we may be building intimacy with someone. The pace of our auditory digital world often means we 'self' struggle to keep up with subtle communication signals and underlying messages that lie through beneath the tone of emails, text messages and social media comments. Feeling the intention behind any form of communication is vitally important in protecting the self and maintaining your boundaries. The art of using the range of emotional senses that we have is being left behind, and real connection to self, people and our communities is being lost. Uncle Lewis shares that Aboriginal people's eyesight and hearing were exceptional. The ability to connect with heart, mind and hands, and their awareness of their environment (Country) allowed a high level of skill in cultivating consciousness of 'self' and the ability to travel across Country in a highly advanced manner, so as to remain in harmony.

At the time of the Industrial Revolution, adults and children worked long hours in the 'doing', with little time in our natural 'being' state. Humans have endured harsh environments, but as we know, to struggle is to experience the richness of life. It requires skill to reflect our thinking kindly towards oneself and others, and if done well it brings greater levels of self-love and self-care to the world.

Self-love is an internally enriching experience that contributes to greater levels of the sense of fulfilment and contentment that resides in one's mind and heart. The concept of our mind and heart working in harmony can bring the self to a wholistic experience. The 'Dream State' is often discussed in First Nations culture; to live in 'Dreamtime' has many interpretations, and scholars have many views on this subject. We are made up of many stories. Some are positive, enriching experiences, while others may be full of heartache, pain, suffering and learning opportunities. What works and what doesn't work for us and the self? When we reflect, we have the ability to bring meaning to these experiences and how they have shaped us as we have taken the learnings and feedback to our higher self for growth. This process brings healing and ultimately brings us back to our wholeness. Taking ourselves back to wholeness, seeing clearly who we are and where we are at any given point in time in our life, is a beautiful gift.

On the journey of life, when we give permission to ourselves to pause and embrace stillness, it is a truly wonderful gift. A moment of sacredness is being cultivated. My learnings and understanding of the First Nations concept of 'living on Country' is a sacred experience. David Suzuki's book *Wisdom of the Elders* provides further insights into the concept of Sacred Balance, or how we see our people and the Earth working as one.

Let us draw on this concept of men and women, or the masculine and feminine, working in harmony as one. When we witness this value in ourself, when we can be alive and wake up every morning recognising that it is a sacred moment and a gift, we begin to see gratitude for the greater collective. The pace of life can be hectic and we often struggle to find the space to bring all our thoughts back to whole. If we find rituals in our morning or evening to collect these stories and experiences and bring them back to whole, love for our truest nature of 'self' shines for the benefit of everyone. A new day is born.

66 Without suffering, there's no happiness. So, we shouldn't discriminate against the mud. We have to

learn how to embrace and cradle our own suffering and
the suffering of the world, with a lot of tenderness.
No Mud, No Lotus, **Thich Nhat Hanh**

Self-kindness or in 'Emu dreaming liking yourself' for me is being
okay some mornings with sleeping in, not always getting up before
the sunrise. It is being okay with not having to perform seven days
a week, being okay and accepting myself for who I am. Self-love is
acceptance that I can be lazy some days. Laziness often allows us
the space in our physical and emotional world, in which to ponder
about self and be okay with where we are at in life. When we listen
deeply to ourself, we are able to see what works best for ourself in a
given period of time in our life. Sometimes words or phrases we use
don't really describe what the 'self' is trying to say. Western cultures
sometimes have a negative view on what being lazy really means.
But the word 'lazy' might mean giving permission to rest at home,
and ease up the pace of life so we can cultivate a healthy perspective on life. Uncle Steve Goldsmith would enrich audiences with
stories of the pre-trouser days and being okay sometimes with being
lazy around the home.

Morning meditation and finding some space to ponder who you
have become is a simple gift. You give permission to yourself amongst
the noise of life. Finding a new routine in my early morning to
schedule in quiet time provides more the opportunity for self-reflection on what is important. Amongst schedules, competing priorities
and an external world full of pressure, how to be the best I can for
myself is explored best before the sun comes up.

Stillness of self is to be explored safely. The 'plane of possibility'
described in Daniel Siegal's book *Aware* explores the concept of a
'wheel of awareness in a meditation practice', looking at how the
mind works on the plane and a meditation practice that cultivates

peace, focus and presence. If we begin each day with an intention to live life with kind thoughts to ourselves and extend this to others, think how we will transform what we have into a collective world. The concept of loosening our grip on the idea that self is separate to others and Mother Nature is fascinating.

It is an interesting insight that the mind sits outside our brain. For thousands of years yogis have sat with breath and cultivated a beautiful mind. If the mind sits outside the brain, we can bring awareness that we are one. The yoga community have been teaching the concept of unity and oneness for thousands of years. It is a beautiful concept, but more so a recognition that we all belong on this planet together. I was introduced to a concept called the 'butterfly model': what happens in one part of the world will have an impact on the other side of the world. This is the same idea as the duality concept or, as Uncle Lewis describes it as *Yara*. When we add *Par* – Equal, that is everything is equal in the universe we are able to see *truth* more clearly and break down complexity and bring simplicity into our life and world.

If we are cultivating our true self, then self-love is recognising we all wish to seek connection. To connect to our truest nature is to be in nature, to feel the wonder of nature and how it nurtures our soul. When we are in love with nature and life, we begin to see the wonder of how we respond, act and behave in our environment. To savour these moments of self in nature is to enjoy the moment to the full.

The following are some suggestions for ways to encourage the man, or the masculine, to live deeply.

Para Yoga Practice

Para: Vedic terminology. Far, distant, remote (in space), opposite, ulterior, farther that, beyond, on the other or farther side of. Ancient past, later, following, succeeding, subsequent. Final, last.

Wonder and awe are power sources that propel us to live deeper, to enquire: *What is the world made out of? What is my body made out of?* Para Yoga is a technique in which you take any element of your body and develop a subtler and subtler (*suksma-suksma*) appreciation of all its levels, until you perceive its foundation, its ultimate reality (*para*), the source of existence. One of the skills here is to find what fascinates you so deeply that you want to go in and spend time meditating in this way. When you discover an element that intrigues you, engage with it using all your senses and instincts. If you suddenly fall in love with the element of water, pay special attention when drinking anything, bathing, walking in the rain, watering the plants or swimming. Absorbing our senses into things that we seek allows greater levels of the love within our self and the world we live within.

Heart Mind Breath Cultivation

I have seen cold smouldering smoke when on Country watching the misty sunrise, and heard the noise of birds, and felt the morning heat of the day warm up the land quickly.

Pause, reflect and listen to self, how it sits in nature and place, absorbing what self is required to do for the day, whilst enjoying the stillness and no movement. Have gratitude to be up early before others quickly move through the day. In doing so, you see yourself clearly, removing the fog from your mind.

Observe the breath through the nose, and be disassociated from all experiences that have existed and sit within your memory. It is an achievement on the pathway towards bliss when you build the muscle of stillness of your thoughts. Like anything in life, it takes time to nurture stillness in life. To collect your thoughts and bring forth wholeness is to reach a moment of love in one of your experiences.

How wonderful when you listen to yourself and the collective experiences that have captured your consciousness.

The plane of possibility is an interesting concept for how the mind works to extend its manifestation capabilities and to heal what is seen. Love is endless and beyond measure when you recognise the true nature of love. When it's not love and it is serving another value, you must act within your capacity to serve however you can. Love is a value and is expansive to self and others; recognise this and contribute where you can. When our community or networks begin to recognise this expansiveness of love, we will begin to transcend others and see our 'tribes' influence a particular message to be shared with the greater world.

The heart is a vibrating vessel in the body, and the mind transmutes thoughts into actions for the body. When we cultivate coherence between heart and mind and move forward in life, our doing, action and tasks are achieved with greater clarity, ease and momentum.

Meditation and Mindfulness

We carry inside us so many different parts, stories and mixed messages that we seek meaning in order to make sense of what is important for ourself as we navigate the world. When we have a wave of ongoing thoughts that flows from an enriching day of fullness and abundance, it will transform us and we will grow with greater speed, but only if we bring awareness to those enriching experiences. This is the benefit of daily meditation: it also brings an enriched life.

My interest in meditation first took hold of me when I was in remote outback Northern Territory sitting next to an old fella. For two days I was being patient while my car was being fixed. I reflect further, and recall sitting on the beach while on surf patrol, soaking in the sand and water, or waiting in the marshalling area at a surf carnival for my next surf race; with a towel over my head, I visualised myself remaining calm and in-focus, and how I wished to feel during the Iron Man race that was fast approaching. We can partially go into a meditative state and still have awareness. Competing all day in surf races takes a physical toll on your overall wellbeing, so it was important to keep myself optimally chilled but still in the zone for the next surf race. The Iron Man multi-disciplinary endurance event was the most gruelling event after competing in 12+ races throughout the day. So, at surf carnivals I would sit on the beach and be in a meditative state, slowing my heart rate down.

I had other techniques for staying in the zone. Under the beach towel in the event-marshalling space, I would play with the sand, letting it run through my hands. I could rest my mind in this mindfulness space of sand moving through my fingers. High performance brings a feeling of intensity, so it was important to seek balance. The calmness I felt as sand was running between my fingers and hands allowed my mind to be distracted slightly from the feeling that I was about to endure in the next surf race. Being mindful of the texture of the sand absorbing sand-granules easily slipping through my fingers, I could easily get lost in the moment. If you know when to use rest periods for your mind, and are aware of when your mind will need to perform, you will be more effective in many aspects of life.

If used effectively and consistently, meditation and mindfulness can assist us in all areas of our life, not just in the sporting arena. The mind and the thinking brain have many roles and thinking styles, so having a range of meditation practices will support the diversity of your life and strengthen the whole of your being. Some common meditation practices include: mindfulness, focused or Zen style, movement/walking, mantra, transcendental, loving kindness, visualisation and vipassana meditation.

When you build mind muscle for a particular need or area within your life, you can achieve greater levels of fulfilment, clarity and outcomes in a different area of your life. The mind is a wonderful and incredible tool for achieving what you strive towards. What you focus on, you manifest. If it's loving relationships and a happier and more contented life, then having a loving kindness meditation practice will promote a kinder relationship with self and others.

Loving Kindness Meditation for Men

The dialogue occurring inside your mind and the little voice or inner critic that you listen to can often determine how you behave and act in the external world. To still this voice, try this mediation.

- Sit somewhere comfortably.
- Close your eyes gently. Feel your breath flowing through your nose, in and out like a gentle wave on the shoreline. Let the breath find its own rhythm, then with awareness allow the breath to settle more softly into an even, slow in-and-out cycle.
- In your inner thoughts, say hello to yourself kindly. *G'day, Jim, how are you?*
- Place your hand over your heart.
- Say these words softly to yourself:
  - May I be happy
  - May I be grateful
  - May I be kind to myself
  - May I be full of love
  - May I be peaceful
  - May I be healthy
  - May I live well and with ease, with myself and others.

- Repeat several times, with intentional kindness to yourself.
- Finally, take a few breaths and just rest quietly in your own body, accepting that what you experience is exactly as it is, and be okay with what will be for you on this day. Remain silent, continue to breathe, and if you feel you need to repeat these words, do so.

Source: *The Mindful Self-Compassion Workbook*,
Dr Kristin Neff, PhD

To Be Nurtured Back to Whole, the Self Needs Nature

Our life has many rivers and stories that shape us and take us in different directions. Life Coaching has a range of beautiful tools to take us back to the whole of our natural being. The Wheel of Life is a wonderful model that looks at the self and how it navigates all elements within, as it takes on the different parts of the journey of life. A model like the Wheel of Life allows us to check in regularly to see if any of the wheel does not seem quite right.

The Tree of Life is another beautiful model that allows us to stand strong with roots grounded in the soil, as our life extends like the many growing branches reaching out. The leaves, blossom and flowers at the end of the branches represent the joy and success of your journey for personal growth, and standing strong in your truth and who you are.

Coaching looks at the different values that drive us and shape our being and who we want to become. What if there was one value that we all can embrace, which could shape all of us, and keep us all moving in the right direction and caring for our people and the planet? Could this be wellbeing? Nature is nurturing, and our essential nature is to care for ourself so we can care for others. Today we recognise that our environment – Planet Earth, our home – needs to be cared for as much as ourselves. Does it not?

Virtues vs Values

Shakti Durga {www.shaktidurga.com) teaches the importance of Virtues through her devotion and study, which promote Virtues and her 'School for the Soul'. Virtues bring us to the realisation that we have some values that are good and some that are not so good. Virtues are behaviours showing high moral standards. Virtue is the quality of being morally good, or moral excellence. Virtue can also mean excellence. If a person who has lesser virtues is able to look at his or her wellbeing and see the whole with clarity and awareness, they can begin to grow into living a higher virtue. Our environment is fundamental to the 'well of the being', so virtues that nurture the being to be well are good for everyone.

To keep it simple: for a better, cleaner life, to reach as many people as possible and bring them back to Country and planet, and to be well as you strive for wellness, a simple virtue to have as a core value would be: *do good to people and place*. A key principle in coaching is bringing your client to self-awareness.

To strengthen and sustain this, we add: *to consistently cultivate awareness in your life, implement good structure that forms sustaining habits and rituals that bring awareness into your day*. Awareness is cultivated through regular stillness, listening to breath, and collecting your thoughts at the end of the day. Our mind is expansive and picks up other people's thoughts and energy throughout the day, so it becomes important to weed out those thoughts that do not serve us.

Early morning is best for stillness, as movement is slow after the body has rested. The Earth and all living things have rested, the sun hasn't heated up the day with energy. It is the perfect time to reflect on self and what you must put in your life, or remind yourself what is important, what matters most to you and the people, so you may serve and be well.

Virtues for a Healthy Man

Virtues build the spirit of man. Virtue is moral excellence. A virtue is a trait or quality that is deemed to be morally good and thus is valued as a foundation of principle and good moral being. In other words, it is a behaviour that shows high moral standards, doing what is right and avoiding what is wrong. 52 Virtues deemed to be a moral of excellence have been identified. The following are especially important for a man on the path to becoming whole, to serve and be well:

Power of Gratitude: Be grateful for each and every attempt anyone makes to help, support or encourage you. Don't push it away or respond without grace. A lack of gratitude stalls friendships, relationships, projects and flow in your life. Radiate the spirit of gratitude to anchor universal abundance of all good things.

Power of Devotion: Gives us the capacity to love with commitment. It is the power that turns the wheel of the cosmos. Devotion creates the flow of energy between two souls and enables the grace and strengths of one to flow into the other. It is how couples grow happily old together, and tend to resemble each other as the years go by. Devotion opens the heart and lets the spirit soar, connecting with the Divine within and coming into unity with the Divine in others.

Power of Unity: Strengthens and expands our consciousness. Divine energy is amplified and revealed more easily. Meditation and spiritual practices are more powerful in a unified group. The soul seeks unity, whereas the ego strives for separateness and control. There can be unity in diversity, as long as our spirits remain united.

Power to Love: Enables us to open our hearts and experience the wonder of unity and connectedness to others. It changes us, challenges us and defines us. Our minds, hearts and souls become attuned and we merge in transformative and illuminating being-ness. Right action flows from the power to love, and when we love unconditionally, we open to the world of the miraculous.

Power of Humility: When we embrace true humility, we move out of our ego and into a surrendered state of grace. We neither doubt our worth nor need arrogance as a false support. The power of humility helps us find our inner truth and is an attribute of those who are divinely self-realised.

Power of Courage: Is the enabling power of a brave heart. It enables us to face and defeat our fears. Fear guards the doorway to many wonderful things including adventure, success and love. Courage lets us walk on through. With courage we can reassess our lives, make changes, meet challenges, assert our truth, follow our guidance, climb mountains and forge our way in the world. The power of courage enables us to be true to our inner calling and lead a principled life.

The Eight Limbs of Yoga

On the path to a better life for man and woman, the Eight Limbs of Yoga outline the body as our vessel, allowing us to transform and purify the physical body and energy body, gain mastery over sense, and become free from worldly illusions. The ultimate goal of practising the Eight Limbs of Yoga is to achieve self-realisation.

These are the Eight Limbs of Yoga:
1. YAMA – Restraints, moral disciplines or moral vows
2. YIYAMA – Positive duties or observances
3. ASANA - Posture
4. PRANAYAMA – Breathing techniques
5. PRATYAHARA – Sense withdrawal
6. DHARANA – Focused concentration
7. DYANA – Mediation absorption
8. SAMADHI – Bliss or enlightenment.

The Australian Man

Footy, surf club a bit of cricket, down the beach for a surf or down the pub – this is our typical stereotype of the Aussie male. We have travelled some distance, with multiculturalism shaping aspects of the Australian culture. Physical activity is still a strong component of our Australian society, and a sportsman is highly valued and a role model for many men and communities across the land. Emotional wellbeing is less a priority, particularly for men. However, this is changing for the better. We give our cars a tune-up so they perform well on the road, so why not ourselves? More and more men are taking up the challenge and the month of November is now dedicated to men's health.

In thinking about men's health, I explored the concept of men embracing the matriarch some years ago. The matriarch is a governance and social structure that recognises the woman or the feminine role in leadership across business and community sectors. The feminine and masculine both have traits that do not serve our families and communities and building loving relationships. Toxic masculinity, as described by many writers, has become a problem for our society, crippling family structures and the wellbeing of men – or, if we look at it more closely, anyone expressing unhealthy masculinity, be it a woman or a man. Within the diverse families of our society, we need to lean more into fatherhood or parenting boys and girls in a way that allows each child to explore their feelings. We need to equip boys and girls with the skills to manage their emotions in a healthy manner, so they can experience both healthy masculine and feminine energy.

There are also behavioural traits of unhealthy or excessive feminine energy. They include feeling too sheltering towards others' wellbeing, which will manifest as codependency, victimhood and lacking in emotional intelligence.

Domestic violence is a symptom of people not understanding how to have a loving relationship with self and a partner. Sadly, within our schools we have not been traditionally been taught self-awareness and skills in personal development, how to navigate social skills, self-management, boundaries and emotional needs.

The story of how we see Australian men within our society has been shaped by a concept called 'tribal groups', which is found in sporting groups and clubs, on television, in schools and many sub-cultures and personal interest groups across our communities. Sometimes we label all men as tough beer-drinking blokes who don't cry, and suck up their feelings whilst standing around the Australian BBQ talking with friends. As a multi-cultural society, we have many ethnic and culturally rich communities with enriching stories that form their cultural beliefs and values. Today we see more interweaving of beliefs and values, and an evolving culture that is always leaning into what is best for people and the planet. First Nations culture is the first to recognise how best we can embrace what is best for the wellbeing of Country and people.

Uncle Steve Goldsmith was a wonderful 'cultural warrior' but sadly, like many Aboriginal men, he passed away far too early in life. An ambassador for Aboriginal cultural and Australia, Steve would always remind others that 'our people have always welcomed people around the camp fire'. Uncle Steve was the first to reference this term and the concept of 'Indigeneity'.

The last time I saw Uncle Steve was outside the South Australia Migration Museum during NAIDOC week. We spoke at length about food on Country, and he asked about my son Logan. I mentioned that Logan was studying at Adelaide University, 500 metres away from where we were, in the fields of music and sound engineering. Uncle Steve, the great collaborator that he was, suggested he connect Logan with the School of Indigenous Languages at Adelaide University. He was always looking to weave threads together and join the dots so we could share and keep this beautiful culture alive for all of us. Fittingly Uncle Steve's totem was the native bee.

The word 'Indigeneity' refers to the fact of originating or occurring naturally in a particular place. In the phrase 'collective rights based on the indigeneity of the community', Steve used the word to encourage all Australians to work on things and tackle our collective problems together. I reflect back on Uncle Steve as a man and see him clearly as a 'cultural coach on Country', the great collaborator who focused on bringing people together for good.

Who do we want to become, as the individual and as the group? Every sub-culture in a society has a set of values, norms and particular beliefs that exist within the group. The group or sub-culture has a belief in something bigger than the individual, perhaps how we should live on country, a set standard that tells us how to behave in this group.

Growth within self is important if you are to have an abundant and enriching life. Traditionally, working men have always been involved in the doing, action, task-focused, physical and office work that is productive, and held values that had high expectations of performance and outcomes. Society (tribal groups) has expectations around measurement of key performance indicators, profit-driven results and performance around Gross Domestic Product (GDP).

Some men don't spend much time nurturing themselves, reflecting on what's important and how to manage themselves, their feelings and emotions, and feeling their authentic self. But checking in with themselves is another form of growth, growing the heart muscle and range of feelings. We need to be cultivating 'heart men' who are emotionally wise and stand strong in our community as sound and wise leaders. I put forward this vision for enriching our men and the masculine to stand equally next to the women and all that the feminine is. In the history of humanity, this vision has never been so important as in today's challenging world, where we face some of our biggest global and local problems on the horizon.

Body Scan Exercise

This is a simple yoga 'nidra' meditation for men:
- Find a comfortable place - it could be sitting in the car or finding a nature park, for example. Bring awareness to breath, closing eyes softly and set an intention. Set an intention for this exercise. An intention is something that you want to achieve inside you that is troubling you or a feeling emotion

that may be stuck in a part of your body and you wish to release this feeling as it no longer serves you.

- Close your eyes and listen to your breath for a few minutes. Say the words: *I am whole and I wish to release parts of my body and bring them back to my whole body as one.*
- Repeat this several times and feel what comes through your body, allow yourself the time and patience to feel these feelings throughout your body. Find some intimacy with yourself and these feelings and be okay with your internal conversation with yourself. Say kind words to your inner self.
- After you have repeated this several times, ensure you keep your eyes closed and place your hand on your heart and visualise scanning yourself. Begin at the base at your feet and the base of your body, allow to move your internal vision upwards into your heart, throat, arms and head sending your thoughts into your crown chakra and connecting to a bright light above your head.
- Repeat this a second time to allow you to move through this feeling of wholeness. Once completed open your eyes slowly and resting in stillness for a few minutes and notice what thoughts and feelings arise within your body.

You may need to practise this regularly in your daily routine and allow the benefits to work through into your body. Enjoy!

Self-Awareness

Having self-awareness means that you have a sharp realisation of your personality, including your strengths and weaknesses, your thoughts and beliefs, your emotions, and your motivations. If you are self-aware, it is easier for you to understand other people and detect how they perceive you in return. Many people assume that they have a healthy sense of self-awareness, but it is best to look at where you fall on a relative scale compared to others.

Being aware creates an opportunity to make changes in one's behaviour and beliefs.

While you develop self-awareness, your thoughts and interpretations will begin to change. This change in mental state will also alter your emotions and increase your emotional intelligence, which is an important factor in achieving overall success. ...It helps you pinpoint your passions and emotions, and how your personality can help you in life. You can recognise where your thoughts and emotions are leading you, and make any necessary changes.

> " Once you are aware of your thoughts, words, emotions, and behaviour, you will be able to make changes in the direction of your future.
> **Source: *What is Self-Awareness***
> **www.medium.com**

With self-awareness you might, for example, learn the differences between a realist and a visionary person or another way to see yourself. Do you often chunk up with how you see the world or chunk down into too much detail? This will help you understand yourself.

Self-awareness was first theorised in 1972 by Duval and Wicklund in their book A Theory of Objective Self-Awareness. This book argues that if we focus our attention inwardly, we tend to compare our behaviour in the current moment to our general standards and values. This triggers a state of impartial self-awareness.

Source: *Self-Awareness Can Change Your Life*
www.koutourevent.com

Put more plainly: self-awareness can be best viewed from the stand-point of personal development. It typically means having a deep understanding of your values, strengths, weakness, habits, and your 'why'. While you accept your faults, you are also constantly focusing on different strategies for self-improvement.

> Self-awareness is a vital first step in taking control of your life, creating what you want, and mastering your future. Where you choose to focus your energy, emotions, personality, and reactions determines where you will end up in life.
>
> When you are self-aware, you can see where your thoughts and emotions are guiding you. It also allows you to take control of your actions so you can make the necessary changes your emotions, your behaviour, or your personality to get the outcomes you desire.
>
> **Source: www.developgoodhabits.com**

Until you achieve this, you will have a hard time making changes in the direction your life is taking you. Learning how to become more self-aware is an important skill for many different careers. But here are a few areas where developing this trait can have a positive long-term impact.

Leadership

You can't be an effective leader without being able to answer the *"what is self-awareness?" question.* It provides the necessary base for having strong character, creating the ability to lead with purpose, trust, authenticity, and openness. Self-awareness explains our successes and our failures while giving us a clear understanding of who we are and what we need most from other people to have a successful team. It also gives leaders the opportunity to identify any gaps that they might have in their management skills, and reveals the areas in which they are effective and where they might need additional work. Knowing these things can help leaders make discerning decisions and increase their effectiveness in positively motivating their employees. Learning to be self-aware is not a simple process, but doing so can improve one's leadership skills and lead to a more supportive business culture.
Source: www.developgoodhabits.com

Coaching

Self-awareness interplays with the process of coaching. When one is able to gain a greater understanding of themselves through the input of a coach, it leads to self-discovery. Coaching is a journey of self-discovery, as one observes their own thought patterns and how they affect mood and behaviour. Observing one's own thoughts and feelings builds self-knowledge, and doing this with a coach provides an objective opinion during the observation.
Source: www.developgoodhabits.com

How To Become More Self-Aware Throughout Your Life

Look at yourself objectively

Trying to see yourself as you really are can be a very difficult process, but if you make the effort, it can be extremely rewarding. When you are able to see yourself objectively, you can learn how to accept yourself and find ways to improve yourself in the future.

So, what is an easy way to get started with this?

- Try to identify your current understanding by writing out your perceptions. *This may be things that you think you are good at doing, or that you need to improve.* The key here is to understand what makes you tick, but not worry about comparing yourself to others.
- Think about things you are proud of, or any accomplishments that really stand out throughout your life.
- Think about your childhood and what made you happy back then. *What has changed and what has remained the same? What are the reasons for the changes?*
- Encourage others to be honest with you about how they feel about you, and take what they say to heart.

Keep a journal

You can write about anything in your journal, even if it is not related to your goals. Recording your thoughts on paper helps to relieve your mind of those ideas, and clears it up to make space for new information and ideas.

Take some time each night to write in your journal about your thoughts and feelings, and your successes and failures for the day. This will help you grow and move forward in your achievements.

As you self-reflect, take some time to think about how you are a leader, and how people working under you likely view you. Think about what you do to help other people, and if you could possibly do more. What are your values, and what is most important to you right now?

Write down your goals, plans and priorities

Plan out your goals so they turn from ideas into a step-by-step process. Break down your larger goal into mini-goals so it seems less overwhelming, and tackle it head on.

Setting and achieving goals is a lengthy process, so if you'd like to learn more about this subject, read these articles:
- 4 Free Goal Setting Templates and Worksheets
- The Difference Between Process and Outcome Goals
- 27 Examples of Short-Term Goals
- 25 Examples of Long-Term Goals
- 30 Affirmations for Achieving Goals
- A TED Talk by Tim Ferriss on Why "Fear Setting" is More Important Than Goal Setting

Perform daily self-reflection

In order to have self-awareness, you must practise self-reflection. This requires setting aside some time, hopefully every day, to honestly look at yourself as a person and a leader. Committing to this practice can help you improve.

In our demanding business world, daily self-reflection is easier said than done. There is always pressure to do more with less, and an endless flow of information through our portable technology.

Because it takes time to self-reflect, start by setting aside just 15 minutes each day. Self-reflection is most effective when you use a journal and write down your thoughts. It's also best to find a quiet place to think.

Practise meditation and other mindfulness habits

Practising meditation and other mindfulness habits helps you find greater clarity and self-awareness. Meditation is the practice of improving your mindful awareness. Most types of meditation focus on the breath, but meditation and mindfulness don't have to be formal. You can also find greater clarity from regular moments of reflection. During your meditations, you may stop to think about some specific questions.

- What is your goal?
- What are you doing that is working?
- What are you doing that is acting as a hindrance to your success?
- How can you change your process to improve it?

One of the most frequent forms of meditation you may practise comes from carrying out everyday tasks that give you a sense of therapeutic serenity and allows you to focus on the present moment, such as washing dishes or going for a run. I find for men who are in the doing all day, 'the physical task', it helps to stop and take a 5-minute breath/pause. When we focus on our breath, we begin to rest the heart-rate, check in with a quick body scan ensure no fatigue is setting in parts of muscles, then we then begin to build memory muscle with our body to feel into being more present.

Be curious about personality and psychometric testing

Completing personality and psychometric tests will help you understand what traits you have. Some popular tests that are aimed at increasing self-awareness include the Myers-Briggs test and the Predictive Index.

The Coaching Institute (www.thecoachinginstitute.com.au) have a Meta-Profile survey that provides insights into 'Archetypes' and how we perform in the working space. It can be accessed by an ICG member or professional coach.

There are no right or wrong answers to these tests. Rather, they compel respondents to think about a set of traits or characteristics that closely describe them relative to other people.

Ask trusted friends to describe you

How are we supposed to know what other people think of us? We have to listen to the feedback of our peers and mentors, and let them play the role of an honest mirror. Tell your friends when you are looking for open, honest, critical, and objective perspectives. Allow your friends to feel safe while they are giving you an informal yet honest view.

Asking deep questions (and answering them) is a great way to deepen a relationship.

Make sure your friends know that they are doing this to help you, not to hurt you. Also, feel free to ask questions of your friends about topics they bring up if you feel you need some more clarity to completely understand them.

Ask for feedback at work

In addition to consulting friends and family, use a more formal process at work to get some feedback. If your workplace does not provide a structured way to do this, try to implement one. Provided it is constructive and well done, having an option for formalised feedback will allow you to self-reflect on your own strengths and weaknesses.

To have an effective formal feedback system at work, you need a proper process and an effective manager. Once the feedback process is finished, it is important to reflect on it by writing down your main takeaways. Write down any surprising strengths and weaknesses that you did not realise you had before. It will take quite some time to increase your self-awareness and get to know yourself better. It can even take years, and input from many people around you. Building the necessary habits to help you become more self-aware can positively impact other aspects of your life, especially your interpersonal and intrapersonal relationships.

Source: www.developgoodhabits.com

Values That Make a Man Whole And Wild At Heart

Wild Beginnings

An intriguing and beautiful story that describes some helpful concepts is the story of Adam and Eve. Eve was created within the lush beauty of Eden's Garden. But Adam was created from the earth itself, from the clay. I think this would include ochre, perhaps. In the record of our beginnings, the second chapter of Genesis makes it clear: man was born from the outback, from the untamed part of creation. Afterwards he is brought to Eden.

Ever since then, many boys have never been at home indoors, and men have had a longing to explore. We long to return to the wild; it's where men come alive. To be cornered into a box, an office, computer desk and domesticated to work of a 9-to-5 routine can dampen the soul and spirit of the beginnings of the wild man. Even now as I sit and type, I hear outside a flock of birds screaming amongst the melaleuca trees as morning breaks, and I immediately yearn to turn this laptop off and explore the new day.

In my home state of South Australia we proudly promote Sir Douglas Mawson, the Antarctic explorer and expedition leader during the heroic age of Antarctic exploration. Mawson, like myself, was born in England and came to Australia as an infant.

John Muir, 'John of the Mountains' and father of the National Parks, was a naturalist, author and founder of the idea of conservationism who greatly inspired others to value everything our Earth has provided to us. John Muir said, 'When a man comes to the mountains, he comes home.'

Adventure with the danger, uncertainty and freedom of open-air wildness is a deeply spiritual journey written into the soul of men. A masculine heart needs a place where we don't find digital, modular, online, microwavable, manufactured consent with deadlines, schedules and an iPhone chained to the hand. Where did the great prophet Elijah go to recover his strength? To the wild. As did John the Baptist.

Deep in a man's heart are some fundamental questions that simply cannot be answered while he is sitting on the lounge chair in front of the television. It is fear that keeps a man at home where things are neat and orderly and under his control. But he yearns to be out there amongst the hot, dry deserts, with buzzing flies on his brow, asking the questions: *Who am I? What am I to be? What stuff am I made of?*

As John Eldredge beautifully illustrates a man's wild heart:

A man's truest desire is to find a cause, a battle to fight amongst an adventure to live, and a beauty to love.

Why do we see so many men, including Aboriginal men, lose hope and turn to distractions that don't serve their truest genuine self? They lose the strength to provide, and the ability of the wild side of the self to stay grounded within the presence of the feminine. This is the reality of the world we truly live in. We have dumbed down the man, and created a culture that eliminates the need for the Warrior to thrive, strive and endure the essence of mother nature. Aboriginal men supported the true essence of the matriarch, as First Nations culture supported a thriving, surviving duality of patriarch and matriarch. The concept of the mother and child is the core of a successful society that values the protection of children. But today we see a lack of awareness, in that people do not understand this concept. The western capitalistic society has stripped it away, in favour of systems embracing the patriarchal structure.

Men rarely praise each other directly, as women do. We praise indirectly by way of our accomplishments. 'Woohoo, good wave brother!' 'Nice golf swings, my friend.' Where it really counts is in recognising the moment when a boy attempts to strike his wild side, as his strength, and to embrace the fear of being courageous. If we miss that moment, we'll miss a boy's heart forever as John Eldredge beautifully states. For a boy to become a man he needs to ask himself: *Do I have what it takes? Am I powerful?* Until a man knows he's a man, he will forever be trying to prove he is one.

We need sacred balance between the masculine and the feminine. What we see isn't unhealthy masculinity, but the destruction of masculinity by the patriarchal system engulfing itself, the feminine in confusion with too much of its own ego, and an unhealthy rise of the feminine which may destroy the masculinity of a man who dares to question any aspect of feminism, whether it is good or not good for our society.

The truth is, Mother Earth is sick at the moment, and we are stewards of our planet whether we like it or not. We are not owners of any property, asset or wealth; this is our truth as custodians. We do need to embrace property and ownership; this will teach us to care for personal belonging. The duality of custodianship and ownership is important. One in two relationships have ended in divorce, separation and/or breakdown because of a lack of understanding of the value of duality. There is a lack of awareness about self, relationships and the equal role that a partnership is when it has the duality of a successful balance between the patriarch and matriarchal systems. The duality is out of balance across the world as we seem to wish to destroy the patriarchal system. But we need both.

Good strength is essential to men; it is what makes them heroes. If a community is safe, it's because of the strength of men. Slavery was stopped by the strength of men. The Nazis were stopped by men. Apartheid wasn't defeated by women. Who gave their seats up on the lifeboats leaving the *Titanic* so that women and children would be saved? This isn't to say women can't be heroic. But men today have been stripped of the heroic provider role.

This is even more evident in Aboriginal communities, where the great male warriors and Dreamtime songkeepers of Country have partly been hurt. First Nations warriors would traverse this great southern land on foot, in the heat, amongst fauna that could kill you, across terrain that would test the limits of your soul. They would navigate the oldest land mass on planet earth without a sat-navigation device, start a fire the old way that has come through from the beginning of time, and then travel the next day ready to tackle anything that presented itself. But today, Aboriginal men have the worst health statistics of any group in Australia. The intersection of masculinity and indigeneity, compounded by an imposed colonisation, historical policies that were by definition genocide, that led to stigma, marginalisation, trauma, grief and loss of identity are the key factors that shape these poor health outcomes for our First Nation Australians.

Man is not born into a TV series or drama sequence played out on stage; he is born into a world at war. We need to be aware that we have an ongoing battle with good and evil every day. Living life has contrasts, and we don't know what a bad day is if we don't have a good day. It is how a man recovers from a bad day that is a true test of his character.

Where does man go for a sense of validation? He turns the turno what he owns, who pays attention to him in a genuine sense, how attractive his wife is; to the external frontier of making a million, running a successful business, being one who fights a winning battle, and finding the right cause and knowing his purpose in life. The wounded man, as all men are, is wounded. When we become aware of our wounds with more clarity, we become awake to the truest self that we are becoming. But the biggest place in which the man searches for greater depth to the tracks he follows, is the woman. If his preference is not heterosexual, he searches within another person's soul. To go deep with someone, to take a deep dive of intimacy with a life partner, is one of the most rewarding parts of an enriching life.

Men crave intimacy in a healthy feminine space. If they have found it, they will always provide the space for it if the heart stays open, for it comes into their life when it is safe to be found again. Feminine aspects can arouse masculinity. Your partner flashes a little bit of skin, the bull in you sees red and is turned on for healthy masculinity, and you will climb the highest mountain for her. But femininity can never bestow masculinity. It's like asking a field of wildflowers to give you the jacked-up Toyota Hilux with maximum tread tyres.

They are different substances entirely. When a man takes his question to the woman, what happens can be addiction or emasculation. Both outcomes are common.

As men with the 'masculine energy', how do we walk and behave with a more engaging energy, so that we can maintain our manhood and also allow wild and encroaching feminine to enter our space? Enlightening wisdom with tasteful humour cultivates the heart-mind coherence that enables us to hold a beautiful grounding space for her, the feminine, to enter safely.

As we walk away from the false self, we will feel vulnerable and exposed. We will be tempted to turn to our old comfort patterns for relief. So many men turn to the woman for their sense of manhood; this is where we must walk away from her as well. You must walk away in the sense that you don't need her to validate you, and stop trying to make her come through for you. A women will respect you for standing up to her. Release her as the object of your anger. Repentance for a driven man means you become kind. I have seen and coached many men that have the woman in their life as their sole mission, men for whom the feminine is the centre of the universe. A man needs a much bigger orbit than a woman. He needs a mission, a life purpose; and he needs to know and own his name.

Empowered relationships between two people enable growth. Genuine, loving self-growth is the potential benefit of a relationship between two people. Only then is a man fit for a woman, for only then does he have something to invite her into. It cannot happen until a man has been initiated, until he removes his mask, to be seen.

What does it mean when a man falls in love with a beautiful face across the room? It may mean that he has some soul work to do. His soul is the issue. Instead of pursuing the woman and trying to get her alongside, he needs to go alone, disappear on an outback adventure, camp in the wilderness, take the ultimate surf trip to rediscover his soul. He needs to retrieve the greater love of his own soul.

A man does not go to a woman to get his strength; he goes to her to offer it. You do not need a woman for you to become a great man, and as a great man you do not need a woman.

However, what we see today is the glorification of woman, and this is a challenge for man. We see art, poetry, music, drama devoted to the beautiful woman. The language we use to describe women can distract a man from loving himself and his own purpose.

'Duality' for sustaining a Good Life *Pa*, (Bar) which equates to a 'duality concept', *'Yara'*. In the language of the Kaurna people of Adelaide, South Australia.

> When people find one thing beautiful, another
> consequently becomes ugly.
> When one man is held up as good, another is judged deficient.
> Similarly, being and non-being balance each other.
> Difficult and easy define each other.
> High and low rest upon one another.
> Voice and song meld in harmony;
> what is to come follows upon what had been.
> The wise person acts without effort and
> teaches by quiet example.
> He accepts things as they come,
> creates without possessing, nourishes without demanding,
> accomplishes without taking credit.
> Because he constantly forgets himself,
> he is never forgotten.

Healing the Wound

Fatherhood is guiding children into adventure, trust, and the true essence of strength so children can feel safe to show up. The source of real strength in a man and a father is being whole. When we have genuine strength, we need no-one. I rarely ask people for directions, because with sat-navigation on my phone I truly don't need anyone to tell me. However, deep in our hearts we have a belief that needing anyone for anything is a weakness, a handicap. Real men such as James Bond or John Wayne have one thing in common: they are loners.

A true man embraces his vulnerability, softens and embraces his wounds and accepts them with self-compassion. He surrenders, he grieves, he lets the universe and the divine light love him. Whatever the description of the universal source may be, forgiveness comes from this. When self-forgiveness comes, we create meaning from our story and embrace our true purpose.

Sabotage, Masturbation and Porn

When a man or a masculine energy can restrain and hold his or her energy, this is showing internal strength and self-love, whereas a primal response would to be seek external pleasure from the opposing mate. In the animal kingdom, if we watch closely, subtlety between male and female is the dance we see in the play of love. When we engage in masturbation or porn, we are caving in to our own self-worth, and it is much the same with what we see when we are attracted to an opposing mate. The game of mating is subtle, and to build love and the respect between two people requires patience. Love is patient and kind and does not give in to itself.

Cultivating Healthy Masculine Energy

66 Manliness consists not in bluff, bravado or loneliness.
It consists in daring to do the right thing and facing
consequences whether it is in matters social,
political or other. It consists in deeds not words.
Mahatma Gandhi

The great Indian spiritual teacher, Swami Vivekananda, said: 'Eventually we would all have our own ideology tailor-made for our own spiritual evolution, suited to what we require to reveal our soul.'

Our individual version of masculinity is a combination of family culture and our previous actions. It can be in pushing the lawn mower out in the hot Australian sun, maintaining a well-kept yard, taking the rubbish out, or simply being present in the family home. I can clearly see how my culture and my father influenced my beliefs about masculinity. My dad was always well groomed, his comb always in his pocket, and he was punctual, the humble provider, and the protector. It was rare to see Dad unshaven or not ready. Being punctual and on time was an important value held as a standard in our home.

I see modern men embracing variations of the traditional sense of manhood from the early to mid-1900s. We see men challenging aspects of cultural norms, and expectations imposed by sub-cultures with beliefs around how men should be. The idea that masculinity is determined by prowess in sport, feats of strength, or owning a flash car is beginning to broaden and to encompass other beautiful aspects to be found in being a loving, soft man. Taking time to be still and finding the strength in our inner sense of self cultivates a more whole man, who is able to sit with peace.

Our collective culture shapes men. The great awakening of men is taking place, to bring back 'peace men' that can walk two worlds.

When men connect with their higher self-whilst still walking the physical demands of life, we begin to see more space provided for the feminine within both the man and the whole woman to freely come out and play.

Cultivating Heart and Mind Coherence

To unveil the 'peace man' that is inherent within all men (and women), we require a powerful, calm, discerning and well-harnessed mind. To be the divinity that we are, we then expand beyond the mind. For most of us, training the mind to be obedient and joyful, still and radiant, is a gradual process. We gently observe our thoughts and give meaning to them. The internal dialogue that is occurring allows us to shape who we want to become. A mind that serves us with purity is a mind that is fully engaged with the world and the activities of the universe. The well-trained mind is a tool to enable us to relate to self and serve others. Mastering our mind is a skill that allows pure energy/prana enabling the universe to flood our field of consciousness.

When we align our thoughts with our heart and bring forward any thoughts that don't serve us, we are using the vessel of the heart to weed out potentially limiting beliefs about us. The vessel of the heart is a beautiful organ in our body. Research by the Institute for HeartMath has shown that the heart is the most powerful generator of electromagnetic energy in the human body. When we touch one another with safe, respectful, loving intention, both physically and emotionally, we call into play the full healing power of the heart.

Sitting with our thoughts and placing our hand on our heart when we sit silently, we are able to intentionally bring wholeness, compassion, forgiveness and self-acceptance to the experiences being absorbed into our consciousness field. Having a routine of cultivating heart-mind coherence assists in developing a 'centred' state of emotion.

This brings us to equanimity, that is, demonstrating calmness and composure, especially in a difficult situation. Equanimity is an evenness of mind, especially under stress, so that nothing can disturb his or her disposition and balancing physical equanimity.

> **"** A fool thinks himself to be wise, but a
> wise man knows himself to be a fool.
> **William Shakespeare**

Cultivating Feminine Energy within the Man or the Masculine

Being balanced in the soul will enrich our human experience and give us the most rewarding life we can imagine. When we access the feminine, we access our own intimate feelings, our truest self. That is, we are paying attention to our real feelings.

How can a man or someone with an over-supply of masculine energy pause and be less in the doing and more in the being? Your masculine side is expressed when you're working towards a goal, making progress, getting things done, and pushing forward. Your feminine side is expressed when you move with the flow of life, embrace your creative energy, dance, play and attune to your internal process.

The divine feminine is an energy, which means she can't be seen or heard, but she can be felt. She is the feminine that exists in all living beings on earth, including the ocean, moon, and trees. She is sometimes known as yin energy, Shakti or Gaia.

Take the time in each day to regularly pause to listen and soften into self.

Practices that Nurture the Feminine

To nurture the feminine, take the time to practise meditation, yin, restorative yoga, go for gentle soft walks in nature, sit in a park taking in the sounds of birds, listen to the wind through the trees or the waves softly floating up the shoreline.

Adopt as many of the following practices as you can:

- Gratitude
- Presence in the moment – deep pauses in your day
- Acceptance of how you feel
- Awareness of your purpose and passion
- Compassion and self-care
- Being yourself, being authentic, feeling love for yourself
- Kindness.

Take note of these simple statements to help you access the man or the energy of the masculine, so you tone yourself down into the softness that has not evolved from our hard-working culture and expectations:

- Man's growth in stillness
- Being in the mindfulness
- Being vs doing
- Task vs the relationship
- Leaving your work behind at the home front door
- Turning off, switching off and being at play.

Working from Home

Today, we still see many working men bring work home in the physical sense; they take calls at the kitchen table, check emails and do paperwork over the weekend. This is the nature of a fast-paced world for those who wish to stay ahead of the pack and strive for better standards of living.

Their excuses seem hard to stack up, as reality reminds us what really matters: the people in our home. And a collapsing society is reminding us that we need to down-size because of a depleting planet earth. We now realise that when we don't have the awareness, insights and skills to leave the work energy at the front door so we may soften into our abode, it's the energy we bring home that lingers. Sure, we serve with love at work if the values and mission align to an ethical higher purpose, but too often we see men broken after working in an environment where the purpose doesn't truly serve the greater good of humanity.

The modern workplace today is a multi-faceted environment of zoom meetings and working-hub places; industry looks to redefine how to survive and thrive, embracing innovation and IT technology. Getting and staying ahead comes at the expense of ourselves and of a resourced-depleted earth. What next for all workers? How do we trade and live on Country?

I recall many inspiring people who have shared their wisdom. My life is my work and my work is my life, and I hold the awareness and presence that I can be in a life 24 hours a day and switch my focus to what is important to the people I serve. How can we be mindful of our current situation, and recognise when it's time to turn off the working mode and turn on the living mode? Let us challenge this concept more deeply. Shall we retire, or live right up until we depart, as the Australian Nomad once did, roaming Country and living a life-style so many dream of?

I recall a conversation when I was working for the Life. Be in it campaign. This was a health message initiative of the Australian government that transposed into a lifestyle philosophy which enabled us to view the 'art of working and living well'. We learned that each could be equally intertwined with the other if we embraced some important values around how to Be In Life. The more awareness we have at both work and in our lives, the more benefit for all: we can serve ourselves with greater love and also recognise how best to serve others. Too often we impose our own ideas on others, and then we bring this home to the people we love, not realising that the flow of information has become part of the home.

It can be challenging to work out how to share our growth with family and community, and we contribute to broader society without it impacting our self-love and our circle of intimate love at home. We must be discerning about what we choose to let in our front door, the values that perhaps don't serve our family, the inner circle of love that truly honours self and partner. Our core responsibilities begin with the warmth of a wood fire in the lounge room and expand into knowing how we can all improve and innovate our homes to better service the collective and the Earth. Therein lies the challenge and the philosophy of how to truly Be In Life for future generations to come.

Our comings and goings - how we travel, enter a door, walk into another room, exist in the back garden, go out for a long drive in the car or walk in the park - set the tone of how we feel. When we enter a room in the home or go to meet someone outside the house, we need to be consciously aware of: Who do I need to be? When I have left my home or office, do I have the ability to turn off the last task or person I was speaking to, and allow myself to be totally present with what is needed in the next room? When we have so much going on in our busy environment, letting go of past conversations and experiences so we can be totally present becomes a vital skill. It is even more so as our homes are increasingly becoming our place of work.

The Australian Males Labelled 'Bad Boys'

Being labelled a 'bad boy' is not helpful. We can look at this as a meaningful way of understanding what is going on in a dominant patriarchal system that doesn't value from the outset the nurturing of the overall wellbeing of children and family. First Nations culture lore ensured both the matriarchal and patriarchal systems support the wellbeing of the family and broader community.

A patriarchal system is a system of society or government controlled by men. A matriarchal system is a social system that recognises women who hold primary power positions in roles of political leadership, moral authority, social privilege and control of property. Today we see the continual breakdown of family, domestic violence, sexualisation within our communication, one in two marriages ending in divorce, single parenting. Women and children are vulnerable, but interestingly men are labelled 'bad boys'. As a society, this does not help our current situation and the ongoing trend. We need men to rise up, challenge society and the patriarchal system, and bring our society back into balance. Too often we blame and gender-bash each other, much as politicians behave in Parliament, or when couples argue over things that really don't matter when there is a healthy perspective to be found.

Traits of a patriarchal social system are labelled 'misogyny', which is a hatred or contempt for women. It is a form of sexism used to keep women at a lower social status then men, thus maintaining the societal roles of patriarchy. Perhaps our society still models the man being king, as in the days when a bloodthirsty man with his big castle focused on conquering in the many battles that occurred in the world. Men have been killing men for quite some time. Do we then say, 'Well, it keeps the population down, and war is good the for the economy'? I think not.

First Nations people understood the concept of 'carrying capacity'. They knew the potential impact of too many people on Country on social cohesion, and they understood and the sustainable aspects of culture and lore on society and Mother Earth. The bush food 'kangaroo apple' (*Solanum laciniatum Aiton Solanaceae*) was used as a contraceptive for thousands of years, often during times of seasonal drought, when the Elders would be aware that hard times were approaching by reading the Country and constellation patterns in the stars. The kangaroo apple plant has been commercially grown in Russia as a compound to use as a female contraceptive.

We see bad behaviour as a result of a system that continues to exploit and go against some of the core values in our society. Our community is desperately crying out for us to get back to basics. The things that matter most are our families and the wellbeing of our children. We are living beyond our means and depleting our resources at such a pace that we risk having nothing left for future generations. My heart hurts when I see broken Aboriginal men lost in an imposed white western culture that values profit over people and place. Culture genocide occurred within Australia when we labelled the Australian Aboriginal culture as savage, brutal and not civilised. Was it not white culture and people, and their projections of what they were saw inside themselves as they arrived in this country, that were uncivilised, that led to the loss of the great nomadic Aboriginal man who ensured the ongoing survival of the oldest culture on Earth? It was a culture that nurtured and understood both patriarchal and matriarchal systems, a culture that saw man and woman as equal, and where community clans had their role in ensuring the needs of children were being met. It takes a village to raise a child. Yes, indeed.

" Ignorant people see life as either existence or non-existence, but wise men see it beyond both existence and non-existence to something that transcends them both; this is an observation of the middle way.

Lucius Annaeus Seneca

If We Must Label

We too often have a tendency to use labels. But what do 'good' and 'bad' men and women, masculine and feminine, look like?

The Wounded Masculine or Man could be seen as:

- Attached to success
- Fearing failure
- Needing to be right
- Aggressive
- Cold and distant
- Critical and judgement
- Selfish
- Stuck in the mind and not in touch with emotions
- Defending self and attacking others.

The Wounded Feminine or Woman could be seen as:

- Looking for external validation
- Insecure
- Manipulative
- Stuck in a victim state
- Excessively attached
- Desperate for love
- Sacrificing the self

- Over-sharing and without boundaries

The Healthy Masculine or Man could be seen as:
- Present without being distracted
- Non-judgemental
- Committed and powerful
- Characterised by deep integrity and humility
- Focused and disciplined
- Supportive and encouraging
- Grounded and of service
- Honest, logical and accountable

The Healthy Feminine or Woman could be seen as:
- Strong and with boundaries
- Loving and supportive
- Vulnerable, compassionate and authentic
- Receptive and confident in body
- Intuitive and creative
- Someone who asks, and is strong with her needs
- Enjoying the process of creation
- Able to relate to others by listening, sharing and creating a community.

Masculine energy is strong and stable, it is self-confident. Masculine energy likes to make decisions fast. It's decisive and knows what it wants and goes after getting it. Masculine energy loves direction and purpose. The aspects of healthy masculine energy that create a good man who is a treasure to family, community and society are: clarity of focus, generosity of heart, largeness of mind, strength of body and resolve, fiercely protective by instinct.

The Masculine and Feminine Energies and the Role They Play in Your Relationship

The following is taken from: Bonnie Sadigh,
www.wheelofwellbeing.com.

Love is energy at its purest form. How your energy creates and attracts love is crucial in maintaining a healthy relationship. If we understand the underlying energetic dynamic of our relationship and work towards balancing both our masculine and feminine energies, we can be guaranteed a much healthier and more prosperous relationship.

Masculine and feminine energy has nothing do with gender; we all have both energies within us. Typically, men tend to have more masculine energy and less of the feminine energy, and women usually have more feminine energy than masculine - although this can be totally reversed as well.

However, because of our upbringing and culture, we were taught that you are either a male or a female. So, if you were a boy and you cried, you were most probably labelled as a sissy or heard something along the lines of, 'STOP IT, boys don't cry!' Or if you were a girl, and liked to play with trucks and enjoyed digging in the dirt rather than playing with dolls, you were labelled as a tomboy.

The fact is that society has separated the two for thousands of years. We were never taught that a female should approach her masculine side, or a male should approach his feminine side, in balance. Characteristically, we were taught that we are either male or female, with no mention or validation of the fact that everyone has both aspects in their core make-up.

For any relationship to succeed, and for personal growth and fulfilment, both partners need to be in touch with their less dominant energies. A balance between the two energies is what makes us whole and sustains a healthy relationship.

The masculine and the feminine energies are like the poles of a magnet. Where you are energetically between these poles determines what kind of relationship you have, whether you complement each other or continuously argue and but heads.

If you and your partner are entirely on the opposite sides from each other - meaning the masculine energy is at its highest and the feminine on the opposite side at its highest (extreme masculine and extreme feminine) - what you probably have is a lot of chemistry, fiery passion and sexual attraction, but not a whole lot of deep and meaningful conversation. If the energies are close to each other, towards the centre of the pole, you probably have a good, stable relationship with deep and meaningful connections.

An imbalance happens when the energies fall into the same side of the pole. Most conflicts arise when both partners demonstrate dominant masculine energies in a relationship. This creates a constant power struggle between the two partners. Both want to be in charge, both want to be the decision makers, and both want to have things their way!

The most stagnant relationship comes from two feminine dominant energies, in which case where neither partner is comfortable in taking charge or making sound decisions. This is when relationships get boring, there is no adventure, no excitement, and nothing of significance is happening.

If a female has more masculine energy, she thrives with a partner who is in touch with his feminine energy. Feminine-energy males respect, and are comfortable with, their partners being in the work force, being in charge, and having a direction in their lives.

In contrast, females that demonstrate more feminine energy are content with a masculine-energy male to take control and be the dominant breadwinner and the decision maker.

Understanding energies, and how they can affect your relationship, comes down to one word: BALANCE. There is balance when both the man and the woman are in touch with their core energies and each trusts their partner's core energy and is okay with displaying their less dominant energy when appropriate. It becomes a sort of dance when sometimes the man leads and the woman follows, and sometimes the woman leads and the man follows. It is about finding that perfect yin and yang, where two pieces of a puzzle fit into each other perfectly.

Now let's discuss the characteristic of each energy.

Masculine Energy – FIRE

Masculine energy is all about taking action; it loves to build, and loves to fix things. The masculine sees a problem and immediately wants to fix it. It's protective. Most women are looking for a partner to protect them; they want to feel safe, and they are looking for the energy of protection.

Masculine energy is strong and stable; it's self-confident.

Masculine energy likes to make decisions fast. It's decisive, knows what it wants and goes after it.

Masculine energy loves direction and a purpose. It's competitive and likes to win and break through barriers. It's logical.

Masculine energy uses words more than emotions, and doesn't hold on to things - emotional or tangible; it can let go very quickly.

Masculine energy seeks freedom. It loves to be free. It loves acknowledgment. Masculine energy craves importance; it loves to be given a compliment. Those with masculine energy want to be heroes. Masculine energy is independent and analytical, representing the left brain. When masculine energy is appropriately used, it is creative, practical, and visionary. When masculine energy is misused, it can end in ego, anger, resentment, and inner conflict.

Feminine Energy – Water

Feminine energy, on the other hand, is vastly different. Different doesn't mean good or bad; it simply means different!

Feminine energy is creative and inspiring. It's the energy that creates life. It loves beauty, and it stimulates creativity. It's nurturing, it's supportive, it desires love and craves to receive love, to feel fulfilled. Masculine energy loves the feminine to be receptive of his love.

The feminine energy is intuitive and empathic. The feminine energy is fluid, stormy, emotional, passionate, and it flows from moment to moment like the waters of a river. Feminine energy craves adoration, it loves to be admired and appreciated. Nothing lights up feminine energy more than to give her a compliment.

Feminine energy is intelligent and loving energy that contains the quality of our compassion, emotion, empathy, and truth. When you are strong in your feminine, you have a strong connection to your body and intuition, and you can make decisions based on what you feel in your heart. Feminine energy is receptive, right-brained energy. Yet if we are too much in our feminine, we can come across as weak and lose our personal power.

Masculine and feminine energies are equally important and necessary. To be balanced, to get things done, and to have a healthy relationship, the masculine and the feminine both need to be present. We just need to realise when and how much of each energy is necessary. The key is BALANCE, a dance between the two, and knowing where and when to use each.

" We are all visitors to this time, this place. We are just passing through. Our purpose here is to observe, to learn, to grow, to love and then we return home.
Australian Aboriginal Proverb

Chapter Three

Seeking the Slow

Gandhi on Values: Be the Change We Wish to See in the World

Values determine our destiny; values are the drivers of our goals. We have many values for the many different roles and responsibilities that we take part in through our life. As we take a closer look at the many values that are important to people and place, we begin to realise that wellbeing is what keeps us on this journey of life.

The 'well' of our being is recognising a core value that nurtures all other aspects of our abundant life. If we lose our wellness of self, the being of what is inside us, the spirit of life and force may weaken its light. We may be born with a physical disability or have impairment or loss, but we adjust our core and embrace life as best we can and move forward with a zest for life and all that it can provide with the 'being' of self. We seek wellness and wholeness as best we can. Our wellness may fluctuate or an illness may strike us down, but we get back up again, come back to our core through determination, and embrace adversity and get back on the journey of wellbeing.

> " One of the greatest tributaries of the river of
> greatness is always the stream of adversity.
> **Cavett Robert**

Slow Living

I have been researching and reading many books on simple living. Many authors acknowledge that the growth of slow living is not a new concept, but one that has been practised for centuries. Slow living isn't about doing something slowly; it is about doing something with intentional awareness and being mindful. When we embrace the whole, and savour the simple pleasure and experience those moments wholeheartedly, we live a richer life. An alternative approach to living in the fast land started with the Slow Food movement in the 1980s. That movement has made its way into mainstream culture, as seen in the growth of farmers' markets, and into other areas of our lives.

It is not surprising that we are looking for ways to simplify and slow down. Many of us are living beyond our means, resulting in energy and resource depletion and exhaustion of our mental and physical wellbeing; depression and obesity are becoming global epidemics. We are out of balance with what is important in our lives.

I would argue that the slow living concept hasn't been around for centuries, but for thousands and thousands of years. Look closely at the great nomads of Australia: their lifestyle and movement across Country was based on seasonal opportunities the land provided, and enabled an awareness of their environment. The subtle changes in climate and seasons were always being observed by First Nations people. Whilst we describe the four seasons in the Mediterranean climate of Adelaide as summer, winter, autumn and spring, the Kaurna (Adelaide region) people have mapped their Country into six seasons. The Yolngu people live in the wet-season climate, as we would describe that of northern Australia. First Nation people describe the subtle differences between the wet and dry; they incorporate the many variations in the dynamic ecosystem playing out in the environment; to move and embrace the rich culture through dance and song that connected to the heavens involved an expanded awareness of the fullness of life. The family and clan moiety system involved a greater understanding of community, and the values imposed by this system ensured the culture lore always remained sustainable and appreciated living on Country with a philosophy of custodianship. Custodianship recognised place as central to how we travel across Country and respect our local environment. Slowing down and taking in the subtleness of life and nature enables us to feel, see, smell, taste and hear all the wonder of life and its abundance. Different environments produce varied demands on the people who live within them.

Today, our Modern Age has brought many challenges. No wonder people are looking for alternative ways to live. Slow and simple living encompasses all the fundamentals values that help families live a more wholehearted life, from being connected to the present moment to doing our best to filter the glorification of the busy mindset that often doesn't serve a slow and mindful way of experiencing the world. Being busy with the online world, and living in an auditory-digital world can take us away from experiencing all the senses and how we connect to Country and people. Consumer culture and the materialistic world take us into the external environment, without the healthy internal dialogue that nurtures self and the inner wellbeing.

Is it good to be busy? Society seems to think it is about success. When you ask someone, *how are you?* the answer is all too often, *I am well, thanks, and keeping busy.* This correlates happiness with success. I challenged this concept, and that is how I was convinced my business philosophy and business name 'Living WELL' resonated with my purpose and journey in life, and the joy of answering people, 'I am well, thanks.' However, people will often then ask, 'Are you busy?'

I think that in life we can sometimes be stretched, but after this high-performing period of life, we need to reflect and learn how we can bring more alignment and harmony in our life. To be 'stretched' in parts of your life is good; we seek growth from these experiences. We can also look at what isn't working and what isn't serving us; so, we may still strive for our goals and aspirations, but achieve them with more flow.

I discuss the concept of 'Rest and Perform' in Chapter 5. It is helpful in achieving our core responsibilities, and creating wealth so we may be well resourced in our 'ideal day' concept and our end game plan.

> " To see clearly is poetry, prophecy,
> and religion, all in one.
> **John Ruskin**

To live simply is to see deeply. There is a great deal of difference between watching, looking and seeing. What is called *darshan* in Sanksrit could be translated as 'deep seeing' – seeing that which lies beyond appearances. Satish Kumar writes about the art of living simply and a calling for a society of artists.

With my heritage, I would look forward to enjoying time at a family gathering, and my father's Sunday roast was always memorable. This is true for so many Australian families, whether it is gathering on a Sunday afternoon, sitting around the table, the Italian harvest table, inviting the extended family, or the Chinese family gathering, in a warm home or park, or the great Australian BBQ. Food brings us closer and enables us to share that common humanity between us as friends.

Food is sacred, and in the culture lore of Australia, to kill an animal for the wellbeing of family and community was always sacred, with a deep understanding of what the animal has provided to the community. In living simply, sacredness and ceremony were an integral part of society, and were interwoven as a sustaining part of living on Country.

Today we are no longer waiting in shopping lines with the arrival of online shopping platforms. Communities have become resilient, creating local art, craft and local food stores. This enables us to be in a unique position as we consider: do I really need to leave my home? Solar energy, waste recycling, homes that can be built off-grid, and technology that truly serves the planet are at the consumer's front door. Never before in human history have, we seen the advancement of technology to sustain ourselves within our own place. Connection to our community and a sense of belonging and stewardship await those who wish to truly embrace the grace and fulfilment of slowing down. Ultimately, a slower pace serves the wellbeing of our children and our children's children.

In a home with noisy children, one practice that serves well is to set up a quiet space for reflection, peace and inner-self work so we may cultivate inner wellbeing in our home. Nurturing this energy in the home is vitally important for all members of your family. This practice is a ritual in many traditions, across the eastern cultures of Asia and India and across indigenous cultures around the world. Today in western cultures, the television seems to have taken centre stage, and brings the family together in such a way that we turn off from the world and zone out, so to speak. To zone out is to switch off in a peaceful place. I often reflect on the harm we are doing to our children with the dominance of television in our homes. Television can be helpful and a learning platform, but should not be confused with the benefits of home-school and the range of online learning platforms we can share across our global community. Television also provides entertainment and it has encroached into other communities across the world. It is a useful technology, but all in moderation.

Being mindful of how we use television and other electronic devices in the home is living consciously for the benefit of the family unit.

Digital Detox

Simple tips and boundaries you can put in place to help you create some distance from digital technology in the home include:

Designate a phone zone: Find a place in your home where all phones reside in one location, rather than having the phone go wherever you go. By consciously being aware of how often you need to look at your phone, you become more in the flow of other important things. On reflection, I think many people don't wear watches anymore and so perhaps the phone has become the new wrist watch, so identify other ways to seek the time. Look at the sun, begin to feel and guess what time it may be; go back to wearing a watch if you wish, or ensure you have rooms in your house that display the time.

Set intentional online time: Give yourself time limits for when you're online and offline. Be clear why you will be going online, and be aware when you may use it for entertainment rather than connecting to people and learning what may be occurring within your community. This is being consciously aware, to better use social media so you honour yourself and don't end up just scrolling because you are bored or seeking external validation. Time yourself or check your device's screen time, and set boundaries around this.

Respect your sleep rituals: Try making your bedroom a phone-free zone for the first hour and the last hour of the day. We need to honour the cycle of starting the day fresh, to honour self and wind our mind into softness as we draw closer to sleep. Turn off all electronic devices as best you can.

Detox weekly: Find a day that works best for you, and once a week refrain from logging onto social media and other online platforms. Instead implement a day of other creative activities that nurture rest or assist with preparation of performance leading into your next working day.

Making it positive: Bring awareness to your online presence, and how you feel. Interact with more insightful learning and fun, and engage with lightness. If you are aware that this is not how you are engaging, ask why you are logging onto these platforms. Interact on social media with positive intentions.

Working Smarter Not Harder

I have always enjoyed taking a break from work and driving across Country, allowing myself to rest and reflect on what is important. Cultivating a healthy perspective and enjoying life is what we seek and strive for. I particularly recall a trip in April 2021, during Easter, after the recent passing of my mother. As I was driving across regional

Victoria, I strongly felt her presence reminding me to always take the middle road in life. It was a beautiful moment and I shed some tears, feeling her spirit and warmth reminding me of my journey to be travelled. I have always loved a road trip across Country and think about how in life we will only pass this bridge once, so we should do it well. Mum always reminded me that we only come this way once, and while growing up I would be deliberate about going out with my friends or spending my time and money on going to the movies, a music show or entertainment. Mum passed on the values of quality experiences rather than possessions for which I am grateful today. Short trips can make the working week less tiresome and break up the hard aspects of life.

However, we work at life and however we value time, we must be aware of the good choices we make. It doesn't just impact our lifestyles and wellbeing, but it also impacts our families, our communities and the planet. What are we here for? What is our purpose? And what are the priorities?

Effective time management:
- Focus on what is important, not what feels urgent.
- Resist multi-tasking and focus on one thing at a time, in both the task and relationship modes.
- Do not rush or accept the busy frame of mind; this creates a scarcity mindset.
- Being clear on your purpose and priorities allows you to do the important work first when you have the most energy. Save the small tasks that aren't important for the end of the day.
- Time box your tasks so that you can clearly identify their duration and better define your capacity.

- Batch similar tasks. For example, allocate going through your emails for the morning and mid-afternoon only. Set aside an hour of planning on Monday morning and Friday afternoon, for reflecting on how you have travelled and any key learnings to take into next week. Follow-up calls might be done twice per week at a set time. Applying good supportive structure that enables a productive environment allows you to clearly set up batching times.
- Seek clarity around your goals, what moves you towards them, and the values required. Understanding projects and tasks across your working week contributes to striving towards your goals. Set up 90-day goals that are achievable.
- Add only small, management and specific items to your to-do list. If you define a bigger task, break it down into chunks or smaller steps/goals.

Learning to Nurture Self with Slow Rituals

When learning to nurture ourselves, a pivotal quality is self-compassion. In her book *The Mindful and Self-Compassion Workbook*, Dr Kristen Neff, a world-leading expert on self-compassion, explores many techniques and skills in mindfulness and self-compassion, especially having loving-kindness conversations with the self. In its purest form, self-compassion is about loving and relating to ourselves kindly. If we have kindness and compassion for ourself, we extend this to others. In some of our communities, it is common for self-compassion to considered as a sign of weakness. Strong evidence suggests that self-compassion develops strength and resilience within the self, so we may serve others with greater strength.

Adopting slow moments includes anything you do that helps you to slow down and feel calm. There are most likely certain activities you do on a daily basis that you will find comforting. When you bring wholeness and greater awareness, you begin to embrace them more slowly. Here are some ideas:

- When taking a bath (or a shower if that is only possible), savour the experience and find the joy in watching the water flow from the tap.
- Go for a walk-in nature, or simply a walk outside, or slowly walk within your house. Just the simple pleasure of moving the body gently can bring all that one needs to embrace the presence.
- Listen to music in another room or walk with your earpods on.
- Garden, read a book, cook with your partner in the kitchen.
- Find the joy in simple play. We are often reminded that adults and children all love to play. When we rest and embrace a little boredom, we can be silly. There is a skill in parenting and encouraging respectful play whilst still being creative, embracing the many aspects of play. Social play, rough and tumble play, spectator play or imaginative play allow us to lose ourself whilst building loving relationships with other people in a joyful, loving space.

'Listening' to Your Body

Tuning into your body allows you to build better overall health, increasing your awareness of body, mind and spirit. This allows increased intuition, which in turn allows you to tune into your heart and honour your higher self. It's important to tune into not only the physical body, but your thoughts, feelings and overall state of emotion, drawing on the wisdom of the higher self. When you become curious about how your body and mind work, you better understand the triggers that have shaped you, and bring more wholeness to your experiences. Our body has memory. That is, the experiences of our life enter parts of our body, and they are stored inside not only our mind but other parts of the body. To seek wholeness and to balance these experiences, we sometimes need to slow down and allow the experiences to settle so we can cultivate some understanding.

A useful coaching model that honours and assists in listening to your body (self) so you may better equip yourself in having empowering relationships with people in your life is the Self-Esteem Triad (The Coaching Institute). This 'triangle' concept has the Self in the middle, and the three sides are Boundaries, Needs and Emotions. When we check into our Self, we are able to nurture our healthy Self-Esteem, and all the emotions that travel through us can be transformed into wholeness, love and a greater feeling of a centred state of emotion.

By having more awareness of the self-esteem model, we become aware of our people-pleasing behaviour and what serves us; and in being more assertive with our boundaries, we begin to have empowered relationships that serve everyone. On the journey of trusting what is our true self, we contribute to our self-trust growing, and then we begin to realise we have the tools and skills to navigate anything that may come our way in life.

Body (Heart) Mind Coherence

When we continue to cultivate body awareness and become better at our techniques through habits of stillness in our day, we can introduce mindfulness practices that involve bringing our mind into a safe heart space. In bringing our thoughts and feelings to our body with good intent, particularly to the heart space, we bring about healing within our body. Almost a dream state of healing is occurring within our body. In reflecting on First Nations and their ability to be in this 'Dream state', I observe that it has allowed them to remain in equilibrium with the universe and Country. We explore this further with the concept of a 'genuine custodian of Country' and what is so desperately required for all humans living on planet Earth.

Children's Wellbeing

In previous chapters I have discussed the concept of children being given an animal totem by Elders. First Nations people across the world have this custom. It acknowledges that we are part of mother nature and enables children to stay connected to nature so they will learn and understand how nature works. This builds the value of caring for Country, and children see that the wellbeing of their environment is important and sacred. They recognise their totems, and in some instances, they may be given a number of totems - animals and plants – which play an important role in the Country or area where they grow up. This concept also contributes to children pausing into stillness and beginning to recognise they are part of nature; their curious inner child continues through life as they reach adulthood, when this inner value of being connected to nature serves them well in understanding who they are.

Nurturing our children needs to include teaching them to appreciate stillness in their day, connection to Country, and to embrace, model and value finding moments of joyful play. Curiosity about their environment brings our community closer to harmony with nature and each other. In bringing those moments of peace when we teach our children this, we are instilling in them a sense of collective gratitude.

> " A people without the knowledge or their past, history, origin and culture is like a tree without roots.
> **Marcus Garvey**

Thirty-two years ago, I was in a small plane on my way to the Tiwi Islands, off the coast Northern Territory. I was fortunate to sit next to Jimmy Little AO, an Aboriginal musician, actor and teacher from the Yorta Yorta people in New South Wales. He was a beautiful man with a wonderful sense of humour and a kind heart. After sitting next to each other we talked at the airport and said goodbye. My lasting impression from talking and listening to Jimmy was that life is too fast for our people, particularly our young people, and western culture will become aware of this one day. We need the Australian society to value the importance of slowing down a little for all young people. Young people don't have the opportunity to transition between child and adulthood. To become an adult within indigenous culture, young men and women would embrace a 'passage' process and undergo a ceremony over an extended period of time.

A Slow Home

Our home is our castle, or perhaps it is more insightful to say that the heart is in the home for all to feel safe, express self and love. Our home should be soft, warm, caring, and provide the space in which to nurture the family that sits around the fire. It would be quite an achievement if we could take across our country this principle of warmth around the fire and nurturing a slow home. Today we see an economy on the march to achieve productivity; we value business performance and seek to leverage our income so we can keep the wolf away from the front door. I cannot agree with some of these aspects of abundance of wealth in all areas of our life. For me, abundance and wealth are the ability to live in freedom, with loving relationships, adventure, growth, and a purpose that we are here to care for Country, that provides the abundance we all deserve. Our slow home helps us deeply connect with our self, and nurtures our wellbeing.

De-cluttering Our Homes

Prioritise the things that matter most. We seem to spend our money on things that really don't bring us much internal joy. It is wonderful to buy children presents that contribute to play, education and learning as they grow into young adults. Make a regular routine to tidy frequently rather than allocating a weekend of turning the house upside-down. If you have rooms that are conducive, allow space for family members to feel they are not constrained by the clutter, and feel and see this empty space as a place to be expressive and expansive.

You are creating the vastness of outside inside, which allows you to feel into the empty space. Clutter has a cumulative effect on the brain and mind. Our brain likes order, so clutter becomes a constant reminder or disorganisation, which drains our cognitive resources, reducing our ability to focus and remember.

When we simplify our belongings, we are able to look around our homes and feel calm. If we are surrounded by clutter and mess, it has an impact on our mood and wellbeing.

Living Deeply

When we honour our self and seek for ourself self-love and compassion, which we will naturally extend to others, we take a journey and we begin to ask what we really want in life. What values are important to us? When we are not living in alignment, life reminds us that this part isn't serving us; we begin to suffer and we tend to hit a road-block in the work or pursuit that we are undertaking. Understanding our purpose, why we do things, what we care about, and what brings us joy, allows us to live deeper with greater meaning.

Essential Wellbeing Tips

Water - Always Carry a Water Bottle with You!

Keeping hydrated is crucial for health and wellbeing, but many people do not consume enough fluid each day. Around 60 percent of the body is made up of water, and around 70 percent of the planet's surface is covered by water. With so much to choose from in a rich diverse capitalistic society, we sometimes undervalue the basics in life. It is a fact that we don't drink enough water. A study carried out in 2013 by the Centre for Disease Control and Prevention reported that seven percent of adults reported drinking 1-3 cups of drinking water a day, 36 percent of adults reported drinking 4-7 cups of drinking water a day, 35 percent of adults reported drinking 8 cups or more a day, and 22 percent of adults reported drinking 8 cups or more a day.

Fast Facts on Drinking Water

Adults are 60 percent water and our blood is 90 percent water. There is no universally agreed quantity of water that must be consumed daily, but water is essential for the kidneys and other bodily functions. When dehydrated, the skin can become more vulnerable to skin disorders and wrinkling. Drinking water instead of other drinks can help with weight loss.

Benefits of Drinking Water

Water lubricates the joints in the body, allowing for flexibility in the joints; it forms saliva and mucus to assisting food digestion; water delivers oxygen throughout the body, boosting skin health and beauty and assisting with skin disorders. Water cushions the brain, spinal cord and other sensitive tissues. Prolonged dehydration can lead to problems with thinking and reasoning. Water helps maintain blood pressure, regulates body temperature, is essential for good digestion, and helps the bowel to work properly, flushing the body and aiding removal of urine, faeces and other impurities, thus contributing to the cleansing process. The airways become more effective and less restrictive in an effort to minimise water loss. When we are hydrated, it allows us to perform at a high level. Finally, if we are drinking mineral or ground water and it is from a good source, not contaminated, the minerals and nutrients become accessible to the body, allowing them to reach different parts of the body. For Aboriginal Australians, spring water was exceptional for the health of the body; Dreaming stories clearly identify the value of sacred springs and the incredible health benefits of drinking artesian basin water. Australia has the largest artesian water supply in the world and it has contributed to survival, especially during inter-glacial and glacial periods, notably global climate change events.

Recommended Water Intake

How much water one needs depends on the climate and temperature, and will vary from person to person according to how much they sweat and how much daily activity is being undertaken. There are some standards and general agreement on what a healthy fluid intake is. For men it is 2.6 litres daily, and for women around 2.1 litres. This would be about 15.5 cups for men and just over 11 cups for women. However, around 80 percent of this should come from drinks, including water, and the rest will be from food. (Better Health Victoria – Recommended dietary fluid intake, 2022.)

Buy Local Food in Season

When you choose food that is in season, the quality of the food is higher and more nutritious, it is better for our environment, an investment in our community, and will likely be organic, whilst supporting the local farmer. It also encourages a local food economy and culture. For many cultural groups, food is the key ingredient that brings people together; it is a fundamental core of First Nations culture. Food is a representation and expression of the flavour of a particular country or culture group. Providence vegetation and healthy DNA of organic food that is grown where people live strengthen our immune system. Native foods are considered the 'super foods' of the food ecosystem. One super food is the Kakadu plum found in parts of Top End Australia. Kakadu Plum has the highest Vitamin C concentration of any fruit in the world. Food that is naturally grown within its environment over an extended period of time, has increased potency and rich nutrient benefits for people.

The city–farmer concept, where food travels into cities, is not sustainable or healthy for our communities. We need to address this 'food factory' system that has evolved from the post-Industrial Revolution, as much as the way we manufacture goods.

Food lore in First Nations culture throughout Australia is a topic of discussion that needs to occur. In First Nations culture, food sovereignty - ie that everyone on Country should have access to quality food - is considered a human right. This was the last conversation I had with Uncle Steve Goldsmith before he passed away. Today, I reflect on my life and fondly remember seeing that Aboriginal communities would always share the food at gatherings. I enjoyed seeing how the children ensured the Elders got their meal around the fire. Many of my Aboriginal friends have told me the kangaroo tail, considered the sweetest part of the kangaroo meat, would be offered to the Elders first. Intergenerational protocols are often interwoven with food ceremony, supporting the sustaining of story and valuing the things that matter most.

The benefits of growing your own veggies include: Less food waste, no food miles, no need for packaging and plastic wrapping, reducing expenditure (money-saving), less water consumption. Food gardening is also good for the soul and encourages families to get back to nature.

Born Free

Every morning we wake with the opportunity to create a new day and be born again. Nelson Mandela once said, 'I was not born with a hunger to be free, I was born free – free in every way that I could know.' The term 'born free' was first coined during a generation born in a country after its transition to democracy, in particular, post-apartheid South Africa or post-independence Zimbabwe.

A true indicator of a modern, sustaining society that values people is how we champion an expression of the identity of self against a national identity, so that everyone feels safe to be themselves. Our self-identity and healthy self-esteem are crucial for the wellbeing of people and place, or Country. Social harmony in family, community and the greater collective of a country is a performance indicator. No-one should be feeling isolated. When we feel happy about ourself and feelings and the state of emotion are valued - considered a measurement of a successful society - we begin to understand why people and place matter the most.

The Bhutan Government measures success of their nation not by Gross Domestic Product (GDP) but a Gross National Happiness index (GNH Index). To be connected as we are naturally as social beings, the feeling of belonging to a community should not be taken away by anyone. Bhutan continues to measure feelings and emotions as an indicator of success in their society; and other countries now take note of this, notably with an increasing interest in Scandinavian countries in 'the journey to happiness' as a measure.

No individual or sub-group should feel uncomfortable about their identity, whether it is ethnicity, culture, sexual preference, religion, gender, colour of their skin, hair, eyes and so on. Emotional wellbeing is good for everyone and Country (our environment). Prejudice and racial discrimination have the potential to destroy the wellbeing, economic performance and social fabric of any culture or sub-culture. This country is awakening to the realisation of what we have done as immigrants to Australia, imposing an identity onto other people. The damage to the state of wellbeing of First Nations people is based on removing their cultural roots, not to mention the physical mistreat-ment of Aboriginal people, and can be described as cultural genocide.

When we coach a client, we always respect their map. This is a beautiful aspect of serving clients so that we empower the client and do not take away any aspect of their life. The map or ecology of the person is their interpretation of the world and how they see, feel and listen to the world around them.

For First Australians, the great nomads of Australia, their 'map' or their reality was in harmony with Mother Nature; they enjoyed an almost utopian experience with song, dance, ceremony and a sophisticated and modern culture across Country. So, we ask this question: if a client or sub-culture is experiencing happiness and joy most of the time throughout their life, do we impose our view of how we should live on Country? The client has the freedom to live their life how they see fit. If the coach has insight or the client presents a problem, we are able to take the client to their higher purpose and serve them always into a space of 'love', so they themselves are able to resolve what is best for them and how they can achieve their journey of life.

Every morning we are in the position to create the life we wish, we are born free to pursue what Mother Earth has provided to all of us as a human right, and to be grateful for our home and all people.

> " A leader is best when people know he exists, when his or her work is done, his aim fulfilled, they will say: we did it ourselves.
> **Lao Tzu**

Dear Mother Earth, I bow my head before you as I look deeply and recognise that you are present in me and that I'm part of you. I was born from you and you are always present offering me everything I need for my nourishment and growth. My mother, my father and all my ancestors are also your children. We breathe your fresh air. We drink your clear water. We eat your nourishing food. Your herbs heal us when we're sick.

You are the mother of all beings. I call you by the human name Mother and yet I know your mothering nature is vast and more ancient than humankind. We are just one young species of your many children. All the millions of other species who live or have lived on earth are also your children. You aren't a person, but I know you are not less than a person either. You are a living breathing being in the form of a planet.

Each species has its own language, yet as our mother you can understand us all. That is why you can hear me today as I open my heart to you and offer you, my prayer.

Dear Mother, wherever there is soil, water, rock or air you are there, nourishing me and giving me life. You are present in every cell of my body. My physical body is your physical body, and just as the sun and stars are present in you, they are also present in me. You are more than just my environment. You are nothing less than myself.

I promise to keep my awareness alive that you are always in me, and I am always in you. I promise to be aware that your health and wellbeing is my own health and wellbeing. I know I need to keep this awareness alive in me for us both to be peaceful, happy, healthy and strong.

Sometimes I forget. Lost in the confusions and worries of daily life, I forget that my body is your body, and sometimes even forget that I have a body at all. Unaware of the presence of my body and the beautiful planet around me and within me, I'm unable to cherish and celebrate the precious gift of life you have given me. Dear Mother, my deep wish is to wake up to the miracle of life. I promise to train myself to be present for myself, my life and for you in every moment. I know that my true presence is the best gift I can offer to you, the one I love.

Source: *Love letters to the Earth*, Thich Nhat Hanh

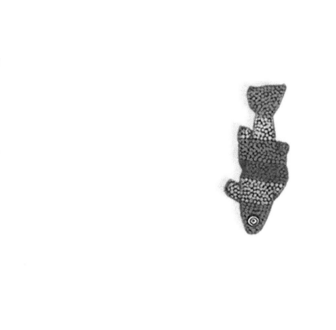

Chapter Four

Trade on Country

Creating a Conscious, Caring Business Sector Trading on Country

> A conscious Business focuses on delivering value to all of its stake-holders and works to align the interests of customers, employees, partners, industry participants, investors, the community, and our environment to the greatest extent possible.
>
> **Source: *Business With a Conscience***
> **www.strategiccrossroads.com**

Our environment creates our being, and our emotions are carried into our workplace or business, which in turn creates a culture that can be effective and efficient or unproductive. Today we value emotional intelligence in the workplace because we see its benefits for the success of conscious business's trading on Country.

Cultivating wellness in our workplace is much like bringing stillness to self, so we can shed and move through feelings that we can slowly let go because they no longer serve us. When we have a collective group of people or work team, it can be challenging, diverse mix of personality types that try and get along with each other. A bag of emotions will be mixed together to collectively achieve some common work goals.

If a work team is experiencing negative outcomes within the team, it isn't cultivating awareness across its work environment. If a business is aware of its importance, impact and capability, it is un-stoppable in what it can achieve as a team. This involves ensuring the team is aware of 'self' and each team member's role in nurturing the wholeness of the team, with a shared vision that is agreed upon.

Our vibration is vitally important to how we perform as an individual and a collective. When we are in sync with our work team as a whole, with shared values and vision, we begin to see the business unit wholistically and we are consciously aware of the performance, position and potentiality within a marketplace.

Consciousness in a business is having the full awareness of all the unique 'selves' at play and then extending the collective selves (team members) to reach their full potential in their respective roles. If team members are always in the 'collective doing', we can miss opportunities that strengthen the collective vision and team cohesion. To allow the business to occasionally settle in the 'being' or what we traditionally do, taking the team away for some planning so they can reflect and share the collective vision will bring more awareness to the business. What if we could do this more frequently and always be in a conscious state as we trade on country?

Work study research tells us we spend an average of 19 hours of productivity time actually achieving business goals. Working from home during Covid showed that a workforce can be mobilised to perform within a different environment. For those who were working from home, I would ask how many, in between work duties, put the dinner on, did some prep in the kitchen, or took the opportunity to spend 30 minutes in the garden and were still highly productive?

If we can share these collective pauses in the workplace on a regular basis, or conduct scheduled rituals, we begin to share the same level of awareness, which will provide insights into each team member's wellbeing. When working in isolation for long periods of time in the workplace, we can become buried within the work itself. If we share more of our work stories, taking more time to talk with our colleagues about what each other is doing, this helps us to see our work differently; and we may begin doing our work more efficiently, less intensely, take a different approach, or see some aspects of our work from a higher perspective.

Leadership occurs at all levels, but for leadership to operate within a work team it requires more collaboration across the employees. For this to happen, it requires a work culture that values staff taking the time to pause in their own work and spend time understanding other team members' roles.

Business owners who work towards growing and scaling their operations so they may work less in the business and more time on the business, have more time to enjoy what they love doing. Why wouldn't we allow our staff the same luxury? To give our staff the time to seek greater awareness of their current job and how they may do it better, we need to schedule some free-thinking time or cultivate greater levels of perception in our staff. If we have awakened staff who are caring, conscious contributors to our business purpose, then we will retain their loyalty and continual service. The incidence of Covid has created a current labour market shortage for some business sectors, and this is becoming a significant problem.

Purpose

The first step towards becoming conscious and successful in business is to have a passion that is on purpose, and then ensure that it is represented throughout your work.

Importantly, we learn that:

> **"** Happiness and fulfillment do not come
> from pleasure but from meaning, from
> the pursuit of a noble purpose.
> **Fred Kofman, philosopher and author of**
> ***Conscious Business***

What's the purpose of your business? Why does it matter? How is it making a difference, and to whom? People don't buy what you do, they buy why you do it. Once you understand why you are you, you're on your way to becoming a more effective leader.

Practice Value-Based Leadership

As a leader in your business, you will be expected to lead on your values. These are shaped by your purpose and your environment, which includes everything from your upbringing, including your education, beliefs and the culture norms that exist within you. When you are aware of your personal values and how they might impact your effectiveness in the business, you are conscious and, on the way, to building a conscious business.

As a value-based leader, you will aim to inspire, motivate and encourage based on your core values. You must be aware of what matters to you – what you stand for. This is having a foundation on which you can engage with all stakeholders with ease, knowing you can make value-based decisions with confidence.

Consider Your Stakeholders

To manage and develop a conscious business, you need to consider all your stakeholders, including the employees and the network of business and industry that supports your web of success. I call this the 'honeycomb network'.

The 'honeycomb' principle is currently used to describe crypto-currency and its advantages in spreading the risk of money markets and accounting structures. How you treat them with your values, and in alignment with your purpose, is important in terms of you remaining conscious. It is important to be aware of their respective purpose and values, and ensure they have a voice and opinion in your business is conducted, because we operate in a whole system.

When we operate in the whole ecosystem and understand our stakeholders and work to improve everyone, we are helping our business also. Ensuring everyone feels empowered within our web of business networks and their needs is bringing more awareness to everyone.

Creating the Conscious Culture

A business culture is demonstrated in the way it behaves towards its staff and external stakeholders. If a business culture is awake, aware and conscious, it promotes learning and growth, it will practice accountability, and exercise responsibility to everyone. Too many businesses overlook the importance of these attributes. When that happens, it can lead to the growth of toxic cultures, which in turn demoralise their employees. In the long run, a conscious culture will positively affect your bottom line, as there is cohesion both internally and externally, and everyone learns and grows together.

Staff Retention and the 'Great Resignation'

Your staff are the greatest asset you have in your business, yet today we are witnessing the 'great resignation'. During the pandemic, 85 percent of employees globally experienced higher burnout, and nearly half reported having work/life balance considerations.

For many workers, it will feel like reaching the finishing line of a marathon, then having to start an ultra-trekking expedition. 50+ per cent of CEOs are gearing up for growth next year. The pressure on burnt-out and psychologically damaged workers is what they are calling 'the great resignation'.

Perhaps because we are always in 'the doing' of working long hours, Aussies are high on the list of those working the most hours across the western world. This movement of labour away from traditional work is not just happening in Australia. We are seeing global shifts in working pattens across the globe.

When we see global disruptions due to a once-in-a-lifetime global pause, we see 'hybrid working patterns' emerging. People have been working from home and going to work in flexible working arrangements that have been adopted by some workplaces for a number of years. Are work teams and business groups ready for this? Teams have become more siloed this year. Digital overload is a threat to emotional wellbeing and is an unsustainable threat to the effectiveness of work teams. The 2021 Work Trend Index outlines findings from a study of more than 30,000 people in 31 countries, and an analysis of trillions of productivity and labour signals across Microsoft and other online platforms identified that a potential 40 percent of the global work-force considered leaving their employer during 2021.

The future of work trends post Covid-19 identified in a Gartner consultancy report, April 2021, showed nine key trends to consider:

1. increase in organisation complexity
2. transition from designing for efficiency to designing for resilience
3. emergence of new top-tier employers
4. (de-)humanisation of employees
5. separation of critical skills and roles
6. expanded employer role as social safety net
7. the contingent worker expansion
8. expanded data collection;
9. and as already highlighted by 'Work Trend Index',
10. the increase in hybrid and remote working.

In summary, to assist with the permanence of employee wellbeing, we need to look at:

- how we engage the 'task workers' in team culture and the value of creating a culture of inclusiveness, whilst being mindful of the effects on the employee experience.
- whether we have roles and workflows that can increase efficiency, whilst systems are flexible so as to respond to disruptions.
- whether we have an overall workforce that nurtures employee skills to be resilient, which will equip business and industry to correct course quickly with the right amount of change required.
- how to build a more responsive work culture and system structures, to increase agility and flexibility and enable work teams to be strong in behavioral flexibility.

Lifestyle at Work

As we begin to see the bigger picture at play, and think about how we can live on Country more sustainably, the hardworking Aussie is wondering how to work smarter not harder, and how to embrace a more eco-wellbeing lifestyle.

Healthy lifestyle and family time is what matters most, right? Certainly, uncertainty has challenged or threatened our sense of inner wellbeing, with imposed restrictions on our normal way of life. Like any emotional response, we have seen the fight-and-flight pattern take hold, with protesting in the streets. Rest-and-digest is probably a better bet in terms of seeking what next and how we can do life better. When we are exhausted or feel that our life and human rights are challenged, we just want to cut and run. The digital economy has certainly placed some level of certainty onto a fragile society that is so reliant on the ever-present auditory digital communication platform that we rely on.

Something to ponder

We are witnessing an increase in the number of business owners embracing a more online presence, which places huge pressure on the digital platforms and service provision within this digital space, and people communicating via their auditory digital senses. It will be interesting to see what will unfold over time if this continues to speed up, and what implications and impact it will have on people and place.

The effect of an economic threat on the fighting spirit of the Australian business community and our way of life is taking its toll. In the Aussie workforce people are working longer hours and completing additional tasks, to keep ahead of other parts of the world.

Emotional exhaustion takes its toll not only on your work teams, but on the fabric of society. As people reflect on the impact of the first two years of Covid-imposed health restrictions, they are seeing that work itself has become a threat to their happiness, health, relationships and outlook on life. Work cultures that don't value the worker with all that life encompasses, and in some cases are even toxic, will send staff quickly out the door - unless we see a change in the way business and industry trade on Country.

Workers are drawing a line under the past two years, and we are witnessing overwhelm and greater awareness in employees' consciousness. We will see mass movement of skilled workers, as many experience the simple benefits of working from home. With parents having to home-school, families have had to reconsider their work/life balance. We are yet to see the full implications of large-scale movement of people across big cities, as they consider moving towards regional Australia and drawing on the concept of the simple life and off-grid living. We have the technology to live on Country in a more eco-healthy way, and in the slow-being state. Perhaps it is greener on the other side and that is why we see people pushing into new networks and new ways of developing trade on Country.

Aussies are a resilient bunch; they dig in and seek a better way to live. As they seek new careers, there is the hope that we will see a caring business sector, as social innovators and enterprise bring a more wholistic view of the world. Time is valuable. We only have the now, and being present is what the 'conscious community' has been calling for, for a long time. We see this awakening reaching far more widely. We must embrace this global pause and lead by example.

Australia, is it not time to 'act our age' and commit to one of the oldest surviving cultures on Earth?

Life is about lifestyle, being connected to community and family. Workers now demand flexibility, respect and purpose, so we can parent children with more presence. Conscious parenting needs to come from both the masculine and feminine. Those who do not meet those needs will lose staff. Those willing to embrace innovative flexibility, team-human work design and work that has high social causes, will become talent destinations.

As we seek and examine what matters most in life, we will begin to look at our jobs and have a healthier dialogue with our inner selves. It is about being truly brave and honest with yourself, and asking: *Is my work meaningful and taking me to my end day?* It is knowing the minimum values on which you will not compromise.

The truth is that our society's wealth is created by our people and the land, which equates to the creation of capital. Today we see a false economy. Cash or digital wealth can be seen as a false economy. It is not real wealth. People + Land = Capital.

As Satish Kumar elegantly states about soil, soul and society in his book *Elegant Simplicity* (2019):

Money is not the economy. True economics is land, labor, and capital. These three items are the foundations of the economy. Land represents the entire natural world. Everything comes from the land, and everything goes back to the land. How we manage the land, trees, rivers, mountain ranges, soils, animals and fishes is the basis of the real economy. The economy won't exist without the environment. Having the right relationship with the environment is the foundation of a good economy. Our people, that is the labor market which means their imagination, creativity and skills.

" We live in an interconnected world and in an interconnected time so we need holistic solutions to our interconnected problems.
Naomi Klein

Change for Good – Slow and Green

As we seek to embrace a more rounded society that values wellness for Australian families and community, many see the possibility of the four-day working week becoming the norm.

History has demonstrated that when economic conditions swing in the favour of our workforce, it tends to pave the way for change across the fabric of our society. Some workers in lower paid and front-line work may not have the luxury to make these changes - or will they? World War Two paved the way for women to enter the workforce. It is also worth noting that the Australian worker is considered to be putting in some of the longest working hours in the Western world, with one in five putting in 45 hours a week. In 2015, the Australian Bureau of Statistics revealed that more than two percent of the population, or a quarter of million people, work at least 70 hours a week. Another 400,000 are working between 60 and 69 hours a week.

We may see business owners having to come up with ways to retain staff that don't involve a pay rise. The five-day working week may well become a thing of the past. It would be attractive to some workers, if they stay on the same salary and are working a four-day week. As we enter a new world, it's important to remember that we work to live, we don't live to work.

Ponder this one also!

Our wellbeing matters most, and we need to ensure that we communicate this message across business, our employers, and even to business owners themselves. How we manage our business more effectively will be important, as everyone's wellbeing has an impact on the overall health of everybody. We realise that when one person catches a cold it can be spread to someone that doesn't have a healthy immune system – an interesting way to look at equality and fairness when we talk about community health.

On a Serious Note - Retaining Your Workforce

Business owners are groups of people working for a common shared vision, a goal that brings money or energy in return for the energy that is put into work. After a while, employees, as we label them, will consider whether their work is really aligned to their values and life-style. *Do I feel fulfilled and recognised for my hard work? Am I feeling as if I want to keep doing this?* Meaningful work is aligned to people's values, although for some it may be a short gap towards something better, and so the work they do is only for the money.

Employee turnover is costly to business owners. Each time an employee leaves, they take a significant portion of knowledge and expertise with them. What if we value the knowledge worker from a different perspective? What if we redefined them as students of life, and equipped them to evolve in their job? What if we redesigned their work so it always remains aligned to their own personal growth? A worker will become dissatisfied if their needs are being stripped away, they are not feeling challenged, they have excessive repetition of tasks, and other people's unkind behaviour is imposed on them. We know that hiring new, untrained employees to replace more experienced employees is like trying to bail out a leaky boat with a drinking glass.

What is really going on when people leave your business? Are their personal needs not being met? If an employee's level of independence or their identity is not being taken into account, this may be one of the root causes of a flow of workers who start looking at other options.

For a leader, it comes down to a balance of valuing the overall vision of the business versus the personal growth of the employees and their respective values. This is worthy of further discussion for those who wish to truly retain workers for life.

The First Step

Assessing the current situation is one of the most important steps you can take towards improving employee retention. Look at the environment and engage with a range of techniques around people's behaviour, team dynamics, what's working and what is not. In seeking clarity about the main problem with the work culture, it is important to be objective. Once you determine what the retention problem areas are, it is important to then determine how you are going to measure the impact of your solutions. The strategy and alignment within your work culture need to have measuring tools - tools that will support your journey towards keeping your staff healthy, committed, and engaged in creating a thriving, enjoyable place where they feel a sense of belonging. Applying and setting key performance measures around employee's wellbeing is a new way in the value of wellness in the workplace. We apply 'KPI's to projects, sales and other work-measures, so why not measure 'wellness'.

Lack of Recognition

Recognising a job that has been well done is a crucial element in employee engagement and retention. Recognising employees' contributions is one of the easiest and most cost-effective ways to improve retention. Often employees will not be aware that a recognition program actually exists in the workplace. Research indicates that a recognition-rich culture contributes to a lower voluntary turnover rate. Salary, lifestyle and work-life balance are big factor in retention; but employees who aren't truly recognised for their hard work are much less likely to stick around that those who are. Building a genuine culture of recognising people for who they are shows a business constantly standing in its truth.

We see some tenure-based recognition programs in sectors that perhaps are seasonal, and rely on community to return to the business. They can be useful but are often not as impactful as others. In a tenure-based system, employees are recognised for the amount of time they have stuck around, rather than the actual contributions they've made to the business or organisation. A large proportion of recognition systems is tenure-based, but this approach fails to recognise employee contribution in other ways. Improving on a tenure-based model will provide recognition for employee contributions in a format that is frequent, specific, visible to others, and is aligned to the goals and culture of your organisation.

To be frequent and timely means ensuring that contributions are recognised in the moment; this is when recognition has the greatest potential for positive impact. As time passes, the window for recognition is lessened in its impact. Being specific is another important element of effective recognition. Instead of recognising that an employee is good or has done a good job, let them know exactly what they did and why it was good. This will provide an example to repeat, and when it's made visible, other staff members are given a model to emulate.

Taking this further, it is valuable to provide insight to employees on how their contributions, and the contributions of their colleagues, align with the company's goals and culture. This helps the entire team see the greater purpose behind the work they're doing, and how each of their unique contributions, no matter how small, helps drive the team and the company forward. When we align true recognition with greater clarity and provide insight into their contributions to the overall purpose, the team member appreciates that they are part of the bigger picture.

Mutual Trust

Too often we see senior management or executive teams not sharing high-level policy or strategic information with all workers. When we examine practices of information withholding, we need to ask: *Is it really necessary? Are we acting ethically?* and *is it hindering the overall wellbeing of our collective mission of business and community?*

When we operate from withholding information, it displays a lack of trust in staff and their capabilities and character. Every working relationship operates on a balance of mutual trust. When this trust if out of balance, it becomes a major factor in employee turnover. Business owners trust their employees to do the job they've been given to the best of their abilities. Employees trust their employer to operate under fair, stable and ethical conditions, while providing the tools they need to do their job effectively. Information is one of the most important tools you can give your employees. Employees need to feel they have the appropriate information to make good decisions about their work. It's not only demoralising to do your work under a need-to-know basis, it is inefficient.

Employees need to have access appropriate information if they are to do their best at work. We need to recognise that everyone is whole and complete and doing the best they can with the resources available to them. But if we have a culture that filters information in order to control, and uses information for power, staff will not trust; and more importantly, they won't have the appropriate information to make good decisions. They need to be intentional and consciously aware at all times, and to trust in everything.

The Speed of Trust; written by Stephen Covey provides insightful truths about how 'truth' with self, relationships and stakeholders within business, market segments and society contributes to speed and trajectory and can bring change, good change for the better of people and place.

Embrace Transparency (Truth)

A way to tackle a lack of mutual trust is to build an increased focus on transparency. Being honest with oneself is one of the most important things we can do in life. Standing in our truth every day and asking how we may do better is being open and vulnerable as leaders, employees, stakeholders and members of our greater community.

Truth Speaking

Indigenous wisdom for thousands of years has recognised the value of honesty on Country. Honesty keeps it real and equal for everyone. The First Nations word *Makarrata*, meaning 'Treaty' or agreement, includes an aspiration for fairness and honesty. Within a capitalist economy, the shortfall in this space has values of deceit, fake-it-until-you-make-it, and business practices that fall well short of their promise. A man's word is a man's word.

"Makarrata is a word in the Yolngu language meaning a coming together after a struggle, facing the facts of wrongs and living again in peace."

Business Congruency

Congruency is an agreement or a match between what is within our thoughts (psychological) and our behaviour (attributes and actions). There are many ways to work and improve in this area. Changing perspective is an important aspect of offering an accountable work place. Instead of asking: *Is it absolutely necessary to share this with the team?* Ask: *Is it absolutely necessary to keep it from them?* Sometimes we might be surprised by how many things are being kept secret for little or no good reason. By sharing information, you will see the benefit in how much the balance of mutual trust improves, and more importantly, how many great ideas and initiatives will come from a more collaborative workplace.

Leadership

Ensure that the action being considered is achievable. Don't over- or under-deliver in all aspects of the working environment and amongst your team. Ensure you are a realist, and once again, be truthful about what is achievable. It's that simple. Don't make promises to your staff that you're not certain you can keep. It's helpful to let employees see the actions you're taking; this is where transparency can be an invaluable asset. As a conscious leader, it's important to be visible and consistently open with your actions and communication.

If you have an intentional mindset ('we can take collective and meaningful action toward solving the problem with creative solutions together') your team will win every time. We have seen the modification of working patterns; more people are working from home, and they are being more productive in their home environment. With the global events being imposed upon us, we are seeing the advent of new ways, to trade on Country, but it is important to still monitor the success and progress of your team.

Check in wholistically with everyone. Look for ways to measure everyone's wellbeing, performance and satisfaction, to see whether the work is still meaningful and everyone is growing. When we have a healthy perspective and feel we are all parts that belong to the whole, we begin to become transparent and more accountable with our leadership; and the leadership then spreads to others, who inspire to lead as part of the whole.

Nature reminds us every day that we are part of something bigger than ourselves, and objectively knowing our purpose in our leadership will cultivate clarity to all team members.

Embrace Autonomy - Stewardship in the Workplace

Nobody likes to be micro-managed, yet too often we see leaders or managers in the workplace projecting their own fears onto staff by digging too much into their workspace, and ultimately disempowering their sense of self-worth.

A micro-manager is a leader who isn't aware they are making decisions to spend some of their own time by digging into the minutiae of the tasks of other team players. The challenge is to recognise when it is happening, and do something about it. The behavioural aspect of micro-managing is born out of fear and mistrust, rather than being a collaborative gesture with intended well-meaning feedback.

It is important to seek clarity between micro-managing and collaboration. An indicator is the frequency and directionality of the collaboration you're participating in. If you do recognise any micro-managing, think how you can alter the approach, to favour autonomy.

"It is within anyone's grasp to be the
founder and culture-creator of their own team,
whether you are the first employee or joining
a company that has existed for decades.
Work Rules, Laszlo Bock

The ownership of work inspires a greater sense of purpose, and a seismic shift in the perceptions of an employee's responsibilities. It's a much more wholistic feeling to accept accountability than to be held to it. Inspiring and supporting employee autonomy carries many benefits and if that isn't challenging to commence a shift into this space. We see this once again as a perspective shift, a mindset. Give employees the room, the freedom and the leverage they need to do their best work and they will do their best work.

It can be the little things that matter most in the work space; for example, some basic ideas would be office hours that allow outside time, walking meetings, allowing parents to pick up their children from school, adjusting hours that meet all aspects of life so employees are living a full life.

Re-Designing and Taking a Re-Evaluative Approach to How We Do Business

In a business culture where corporate objectives and mission perhaps don't line up with each other, there are often certain cultural considerations in the way work values and personal values can get in the way of performing.

Our First Nations (indigenous) communities have a different mindset around working, in a traditional sense. We seem to work for an imposed shackled colonial system, that still lingers on from an

Industrial Revolution system, and still seems to steamroll people and place. We trade on Country and we do business that hasn't valued an ancient system that understands the sacredness of life and a lifestyle that values the true evolution of people and their journey to transcendence, rather than enslaving them for the benefit of the elite.

Within some business and industry sectors, slave labour and trickery were practised on a generation before us. We only have to look at the way we treated children, sending them to the mines at the age of 12 years old. I feel blessed that I witnessed my parents' devotion to my brother and myself; we arrived as immigrants in Australia, a country where we could be free to have a better life. Their hardworking ethic saw my mother pushing trolleys around and my father having to endure great pain because the worker was not looked after. Like many parents in this era, they worked hard to support their children so they could live a better life than they had endured. Yet today we see a continual erosion of inequality through a higher order. Control is at play to ensure the middle class don't impose their ideal, which we all know and believe: that it is better for everyone on our planet to be equal.

The Spirit Level by Richard Wilkinson and Kate Pickett is a 40-year study of why true equality is better for everyone. But sadly, today we still see at play a war against the simple philosophy that equality is better for everyone.

Spirit Level – Building True Equality on Country

A conscious trade on Country - or doing business, as we white fellas call it - is being aware that when we rip people off, or charge a price that is over-inflated, or trick people into working for us, we create a false economy. The core of wealth is based on three principles:

land, people and capital. When we exploit all three, we take away the future for everyone. It is the truth that equality and sustainability go together. We now recognise the brutal truth that our environment cannot absorb further increases in emissions, and that further economic growth in the developing world no longer improves health, happiness or measures of wellbeing.

We are now seeing ways of improving the quality of life in rich countries without further economic growth. Drawing the correlation between life expectancy and carbon emissions, the richer you are the more you spend and contribute to carbon emissions. It is clear we need to move to something more like the 'steady-state economy' which was first proposed by economist Herman Daly.

Since the 1970s, the concept of a steady-state economy has been associated mainly with the work of leading ecological economist Herman Daly. The concept is that natural resources flow through our economies, and for us to recognise climate change we need to collaborate and cooperate like never before. We cannot succeed if in practice everyone is trying to circumvent the regulations. Government policies must be seen to be fair and income differences have to be reduced. But how do we impose this on someone who desires to create his or her wealth? Or is someone who protects their wealth the real global problem? Since wealth is a major source of future economic gains and, increasingly, of power and influence, this presages further increase in inequality. Economists Abhijit Banerjee and Esther Duflo, who won a 2019 Nobel Prize for their research on poverty, wrote in the introduction of their report: "We are living in a world with extreme concentration of economic power in the hands of a very small minority of the super-rich."

The Covid crisis has exacerbated inequalities between the very wealthy and the rest of the population. The world has never been wealthier, with large variations across countries and households. The global balance sheet and net worth more than tripled between 2000 and 2020. Yet half of the world's net wealth belongs to the top 1%. I find this alarming and dangerous. I feel we are at war with those in control in a way that gives them the potential to impose anything they wish upon world governments, through a slow erosion of human rights and the displacement of people who are vulnerable.

As I draw closure on the writings of this book, I insert a recent item of news from January 2022, regarding the breaching of our the fifth of nine planetary boundary conditions. It was not just breached but smashed. This is a breach of chemical pollution and the release of novel entities. There are now 350,000 chemicals in our system, and plastic production has grown by 79% since 2000. The *Stockholm Resilience Centre's* mission is to build a strong scientific foundation for better understanding the complex dynamics of people and planet. The Centre's vision is of a thriving and resilient biosphere that enables wellbeing for all.

The nine planetary boundaries are:
1. Stratospheric ozone depletion
2. Loss of biosphere integrity (biodiversity loss and extinctions)
3. Chemical pollution and the release of novel entities
4. Climate change
5. Ocean acidification
6. Freshwater consumption and the global hydrological cycle
7. Land system change
8. Nitrogen and phosphorus flow to the biosphere and oceans;
9. Atmospheric aerosol loading.

Source: Stockholm Resilience Centre

Yet despite their existence, today we witness many people modelling behaviour that is imposed by the manufacturing consent of the elite, to be consumers and strive for a work ethic as the slaves of a system. For what purpose? To take us away from the core of community life and family values, with one in two families ending in divorce, and clear statistical data showing that unequal societies have negative social impacts on all parts of our life. The Equality Trust, which draws on 40 years of social and economic population research (www.equalitytrust.org.uk), clearly articulates that a happy and well society is one where everyone is equal, and business, community and government work in harmony to ensure that everyone is cared for.

Our challenge as coaches, business owners, community leaders and ethical politicians is to educate everyone that wealth and money do not equal internal happiness. Based on our ethos of freedom of choice and the ideals of democracy, we still see many individuals striving to be the next millionaire; and television and marketing brand our society as if we have an endless stream of wealth from our already depleted Mother Earth, who is screaming out to us: *Enough is enough.* Yet we wish to model this behaviour, increasing our economic wealth at the expense of life and the people that matter most to us. Let's make do with what we have, be grateful for the little things, and be wise about how we spend our money.

Land Economics - Change on Our Doorstep

We are beginning to see future projects based on the size and design of passive housing and smaller size (downsizing). Homes are designed to nurture the concept of 'living well', with award-winning architecture concepts that embrace the inside/outside concept and source building materials that are organic, sustainable, utilise recycled materials, and reduce the carbon footprint. The aim is for simple slow-green living, with a focus on how we spend, and business solutions that embrace modern technology whilst still intentionally retaining a core recognition that people and place matter most. With the arrival of technology beyond our imagination, off-grid living that embraces healthy dwelling lifestyle with solar, passive design, enviro-cycle and water efficient homes, can make working from home attractive.

Modest Lifestyle

Living on Country while valuing a more modest lifestyle is better for all of us. I remember sitting at Port Noarlunga jetty after a long working day on the 'Tjlbruke Dreaming - Caring for Country project'. I was with Paul Dixon, Cultural Officer for Living Kaurna Culture Centre. As we spoke about big homes and the Aussie pergola, he said to me with his deep spiritual warm smile, 'One day we will meet on the back verandah and learn how to live on Country.' A golden moment of wisdom from Uncle Paul.

This was during the 1990s, a time when everyone was building the ultimate Stratco pergola on the side of their house. Aussies want to live in nature. We love camping, but I see more and more people building bigger homes, bigger inside castles. Is this from a state of fear about stepping into the true outside space? Children spend more time on computer screens and iPhone, modelling whom? Screen time is now measured on the iPhone. We are part of nature. To live an inside-outside lifestyle is what will heal us every day.

As we focus on the challenges of a changing climate and an increasing inequity across our communities, consumers are seeking clarity and demanding that businesses be more accountable, and innovative in how they trade on Country. The B-Corporation is a group of people that encourage business groups to trade with more awareness. The online platform aims at making business a force for good, building communities not just profits. With a mission to bring business to be a force for good, B Lab provides companies with programs and tools necessary to understand their environmental and social impact.

I came across 'The Pargo Project', a business in Australia that promises that forever, their high-quality drink bottle purchase funds will go towards assisting communities throughout the world to have access to clean drinking water. This is a commendable example of business adding value to a particular segment of the market. We have seen many business groups engaging in this type of ethical practice of adding value and high ethics to do good, and based on a give-back concept.

This behaviour is easily explained in a coaching model I learnt whilst studying at the Coaching Institute: *The Be Do Have = Give* Model. Who do we need to BE, what do we want to GIVE, and what will it give us to HAVE, which then determines how we will GIVE back or leave as a legacy?

Business needs to look at how we can trade on Country. If we look at our end game in more detail, we will realise that through the legacy (how we may give back) concept, we will transform our economy, and business will transform people.

Healing our communities is desperately needed. The growth of coaching is playing an important role in this space. We need to inspire more businesses to understand and value the concept of a circular economy. 'Closed-Loop' is one group working directly in waste management, recycling and reducing consumption practices. *Closed Loop* are leaders in sustainability and landfill diversion. They are committed to building a circular economy by turning waste back into products that re-enter the local supply chain, eliminating future waste.

A final ponder on the added value in our business model

We speak about the leave-a-legacy principle, that ultimately will benefit our children and our children's children... Is this the real TRUTH, or is it not?

The concept is to give back, in order for a business to find an added-value aspect of the business strategy. If we travel via an aeroplane, we can offset our carbon emissions by paying extra to give towards a group that may plant trees. If we buy an unsustainable product, the business has an offset 'feel good' factor if that business gives money to a charity or community project. Do we call this a 'Sin Tax', paying for an indulgence? It is something to ponder as we consider that a more modest lifestyle will mean that future generations have a future.

" The more you know the less we need.
Australian Aboriginal Proverb

Chapter Five

Performance vs Deep Rest

I n the new economy that's super-fast on our auditory digital senses, how can we perform so we may still experience and tune into all our senses, while maintaining and taking care of all the senses of our natural being? Our health depends on this whole balanced being contributing to greater levels of consciousness and awareness of our environment.

When we master the principle of deep rest, we have great capacity to focus for long periods, and master hard aspects in life whilst having the ability to produce at an elite level, in terms of quality and speed. If you spend enough time in a state of frantic shallowness, you permanently reduce your capacity to perform deep work, and more importantly, you lessen the intimacy you share the people in your life.

Carl Jung, who founded analytical psychology, was not shy about taking time off. Deep work, though a burden to prioritise, was crucial for his goal of changing the world. Deep work is necessary to wring every last drop of value out of your current intellectual capacity. From decades of research in psychology and neuroscience, we know that the state of mental strain that accompanies deep work is also necessary to improve your abilities. In other words, deep work was exactly the type of effort needed to stand out in a cognitively demanding field like academic psychiatry in the early twentieth century.

Deep Work Hypothesis

The ability to perform deep work is becoming increasingly rare, at exactly the same time that it is becoming increasingly valuable in our economy. As a consequence, the few who cultivate this skill, and then make it the core of their working life, will thrive. It requires commitment to depth and to cultivating an ability to produce real value in an increasingly distracted world; and to recognising a truth embraced by the most productive and important personalities of generations past: a deep life is a good life.

High Quality Work Produced = (Time Spent) x (Intensity of Focus)

I first came across the concept of deep rest in some wonderful insights by Cal Newport in his book *Deep Work*, first published in 2016. It resonates, with a 'cry for slowness and simplicity' and modest lifestyle, while maintaining the performance and focus required towards greening our economy that we so desperately need. Deep work also takes us to greater levels of consciousness in an age of over-communication, confusion and a high-level masculine/matriarchal society, that finds itself on a treadmill that we are still working out how to transition away from.

There are two core abilities for thriving in the new economy:
1. The ability to quickly master hard things
2. The ability to produce at an elite level, in terms of both quality and speed.
   Also:
3. Be okay with deep thinking and stepping back.

Deep Work Helps You Quickly Learn Hard Things

66 Let your mind become a lens, thanks to the converging rays of attention; let your soul be all intent on whatever it is that is established in your mind as a dominant, wholly absorbing idea.
Antonin-Dalmace Sertillanges

To learn requires intense concentration. To master a cognitively demanding task requires a specific type of practice – there are few exceptions made for natural talent. Having deliberate practice actually requires a core component, usually identified as follows:
1. Your attention is focused tightly on a specific skill you're trying to improve or an idea you're trying to master
2. You receive feedback so you can correct your approach to keep your attention exactly where is most productive.

Deep work helps you produce at an elite level.

The Principle of Least Resistance

When I reflect on my work flow during 20+ years in local government, 40% of my time would be monitoring email traffic and managing priority emails. You could argue that this behaviour is necessary in many fast-paced business and work teams, but does it really help your work to be constantly connected? In a culture of connectivity, why do we ask employees to focus on behaviours that are the easiest? We see this culture of connectivity play out in our personal lives, where we have Facebook messages, text messages, Instagram messages, and two or three email accounts. We have never been so accessible, and have an expectation that people will get back to us within the hour in our business and personal lives.

This approach propels us to reduce depth in all areas of life. It's easy to remain connected when people feel alone and not in touch with who they really are, in a shallow world full of external shiny lights. The mindset is important for how we see the word 'busy', and in the glorification of self-importance, we often neglect being conscious and present in the moment.

Busyness becomes a proxy for productivity. In the absence of clear indicators of what it means to be productive and valuable in their jobs, many knowledge workers turn back towards an industrial indicator of productivity: doing lots of stuff in a visible manner. The cult and evolution of the internet has engulfed our love of being online, for no other reason than being drunk on sites of no-return. Deep work should be a priority in today's business climate. But for some people, it's not.

Among them, the realities are that deep work is hard and shallow work is easier; that in the absence of clear goals for your job, the visible busyness that surrounds shallow work becomes self-preserving; and that our culture-developed belief is that behaviour related to the internet is now considered good, regardless of its impact on our ability to produce valuable things. This applies to social media in particular; the need to be seen on platforms such as Facebook implies that for some, you need such a presence to be in this life.

> **"** The connection between deep work and
> flow should be clear: deep work is an activity
> well suited to generate a flow state.
> **Cal Newport**

The phrase used by Csikszentmihalyi to describe what generates flow includes notions of stretching your mind to its limits, concentrating, and losing yourself in an activity, all of which also describes deep work.

In his book *Flow: The Psychology of Optimal Experience*, Mihaly Csikszentmihalyi, renowned Hungarian-American psychologist, put forward the theory that people are happiest when in a state of 'flow', a state of concentration or complete absorption with the activity and situation. This approach is seen in the first purpose of the Mission of Sony:

> To create a place of work where staff can feel the joy of innovation,
> be aware of their mission to society and work to their heart's content.

And it is echoed in these words:

> **"** Look for your passion, what turns you on,
> what makes you excited, then you get into
> this energy of flow, pure expression of high
> vibration that nurtures your higher self.
> **Anita Roddick, Founder of The Body Shop**

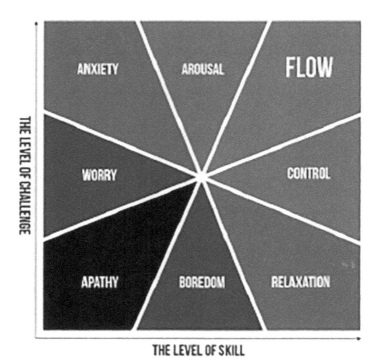

"Flow" chart by Csikszentmihalyi
Source: Wikipedia

Rules for Embracing Deep Work

> " I have been a happy man ever since January 1, 1990, when I no longer had an email address. I'd used email since 1975, and it seems to me that 15 years of email is plenty for one lifetime. Email is a wonderful thing for people whose role in life is to be on top of things. But not for me; my role is to be on the bottom of things. What I do takes long hours of studying and uninterruptible concentration.
> **Donald Knuth**

Cal Newport offers some great ideas for embracing deep work.

Work Deeply. Decide on your depth. The goal is to convince yourself of many ways to integrate deep work into your work/life schedule. It is worth taking the time to find an approach that makes sense for you.

Ritualise. The monastic philosophy of deep work scheduling recommends that you ritualise. Create sacred structure, be the artist and create the environment, and escape or embrace the concept of 'walkabout'. Find the eco-cabin or break away for a weekend reflecting on your life, business or whatever you feel you need to do to increase your perspective on what matters most. Your ritual needs to specify where you'll work and for how long, how you'll work once you start to work, and how you'll support your work moving forward.

Make a kind gesture to yourself; perhaps book an expensive hotel or eco-cabin retreat and embrace what part of your life or business you wish to improve on.

Don't do 'deep work' alone; if it's specifically related to your work, identify who should you involve and sound out their insights and check in at key milestones of your project or your deep dive.

Ensure you clearly identify at the beginning the Wildly Important Goal (WIG) that you wish to uncover and articulate, or express your findings on the project that will be delivered from this WIG.

Be disciplined on the lead measures; being accountable on your progress will ensure you have good structure to still ensure you reach the desired outcome. Allow time for reflection and being lost in parts of 'creative space'.

Embrace the concept of being lazy. When we enter the deep-work space, we embrace a concept of 'deep rest' which will uncover personal insights that aid healthy downtime. The lazy concept is self-preservation of energy to do any form of work. Unwillingness helps us look at what's important and what isn't serving us in a life-work situation.

This downtime truly helps us to recharge energy and clearly identify what is not important. Being lazy can be seen as 'self-love' and 'self-preservation' of our energy.

Embrace boredom. It's okay to just be, as much as you can sit with breath; but if you just hang around, feel your environment and occasionally see what presents itself, the creative mind starts to work its magic. Once your brain has become accustomed to on-demand distraction, it's hard to shake the addiction, even when you want to concentrate.

Don't take breaks from distraction. Instead take breaks from focus. Allocating time blocks away from the internet and other media devices assists in moving away from the auditory digital world and using our other senses to connect with self in the natural environment.

Meditate productively. Embracing a meditation practice and maintaining a consistent habitat in your daily routine will benefit how you feel and experience the richness of life. The neuro-medical evidence supports the benefits of meditation: it helps to focus attention, produces feelings of calm and heightened energy and awareness, can reduce anxiety and the negative stress levels that we may have picked up over the day or week or year. It is widely understood to provide a range of health benefits. Meditation has been proven to not only help enhance work satisfaction, but also enhance productivity and overall happiness.

When you are able to set your environment up so it supports you into a space that is familiar, to perform the task or work to be carried out, you excel - much as in the arena of sport being in the zone requires you to set yourself up to perform. Meditation is no different. When you consistently meditate in a space that supports you to learn the art of meditation and embrace all the aspects in a safe space, you begin to build muscle, going into the 'meditation zone' becomes easier, and you can stay in this space for longer periods of time. Going on retreats is a great way to embrace learnings and go deeper into your practice, so you may take this back to your daily routine.

A productive practice is having awareness of what style of meditation will suit your needs, according to how you are feeling and the outcomes required for your day or week. When you have greater levels of self, you can select different meditation techniques that will have specific outcomes assisting the overall performance and your state of being. Increasing the overall awareness of how you are feeling and cultivating more subtle experiences allows you to support the overall level of your vibration. Vibration is a key ingredient to ensuring you make good decisions, navigating your awareness and being at your best for most experiences when moving forward in life or simply enjoying the being. Keeping the 'bad stress' at bay with a productive and healthy meditation practice will increase your vitality throughout your life.

Types of Meditation

The meditation styles listed below are for specific outcomes. This allows us to have whatever state of emotion we need to achieve a high-performance task or go into a deep state or work and rest. Below is a small sample of what is commonly used today to assist people and work teams achieve greater levels of consciousness in living an intentional and whole life.

Mindfulness meditation promotes metacognitive awareness, decreases rumination and enhances attentional capacities through gains in working memory. These cognitive gains, in turn, contribute to effective emotion-regulation strategies.

Movement meditation reduces stress, boosts immunity, promotes quality deep sleep, and makes you live longer. This style of meditation can also assist with pain relief and also offers some techniques that allow us to see into our future self and how we wish to feel about who we are becoming.

Focused meditation promotes a tranquil mind and allows a deep state of relaxation of the mind. To allow the mind to focus, we need to eliminate the stream of jumbled thoughts that may be overcrowding the mind and causing stress. Focus meditation will naturally increase your overall wellbeing and physical health.

Visualisation meditation allows you to better direct your relaxed mind toward specific outcomes that you would like to see within you. This style is often used by athletes to increase performance, and relieve anxiety and depression symptoms.

Insightful meditation is, much like Vipassana, an insightful meditation that starts with finding a quiet place. The goal is to use the breath as an anchor. The focus in breathing exercises is on the rise and fall of the breath throughout the body. If we intentionally place an experience or feeling into this space so we may gain some better insights for self, during the meditation we begin to see all other feelings and emotions drop away so we gain greater insight into our life.

Loving kindness allows us to cultivate the propensity for kindness within us, so we may extend this to others. This also helps with having a healthy dialogue with the inner critic that sits with us - the internal chatter that sometimes can be not so kind (am I good enough, am I worthy, am I lovable?) can be softened with a good loving kindness meditation.

Skillful compassion involves repeating certain phrases that express the intention to move from judgement to caring, from isolation to connection, from indifference or dislike to understanding. Notice whatever has captured your attention, let go of the thought or feeling, and simply return to the phrases that best serve you. As in all meditation, the mind will wander away from the breath. Simply bring yourself back to awareness and the natural flow of your breath.

The above examples have been inspired by my study and participation in mediation retreats under the guidance of Shakti Durga as a 'initiated disciple' within Australian and retreats in Peedham, India, for which I am extremely grateful. Her details below;

https://www.shantimission.org/

I have also been fortunate to undertake study with Dr Kristin Neff, PhD 'The Mindful Self-Compassion Workbook. Dr Neff details below;

https://self-compassion.org/

Quit social media

Giving permission to yourself to have a break from social media allows you to switch off the auditory digital senses and tune into your other senses of smell, touch, intuition, vision, listening. This allows you to access your higher self. Science today informs us we have five primary senses; if we investigate further into this space, we will find other forms of senses we can access. The natural environment of our other species will access a particular sense for their survival based on the environment that the animal has evolved within. Aboriginal people had exceptional vision, and awareness was high in all the other senses amongst our First Nation people. Today the auditory digital world that is being used for social media is having an unhealthy impact on the wholeness of our being and senses.

The phone allows us to stay connected 24 hours a day, 7 days a week. Connection is part of who we are as social animals, but today we are seeing increasing levels of dopamine amongst individuals, and addiction to social media is becoming a problem for individuals who crave constant presence in this space. Choosing to give social media a rest during the week, or for parts of your day, allows a healthy view of how you are seeing and experiencing your inner world and reality.

Simple steps such as monitoring your use, not allowing the phone into the bedroom, choosing not to log on over the weekend, or choosing a time period of 2-3 days of rest, allow you to be re-charged and achieve healthy levels of inner power. The auditory digital is a 'sense' that we are beginning to use more and more in this modern world, yet it is taking us away from all the senses that the natural world provides for us.

When we go into nature where the world is full of good *prana* (energy), we fully restore our wholeness and the inner health of self. The technique of setting time blocks on social media is an extremely useful tool in building a healthy emotional state that returns us our inner fire of strength, emotional certainty and balance, truly resting our inner state of wellbeing.

Drain the shallows

'Shallow work' refers to answering emails, making phone calls, attending meetings, and other inevitable but ultimately low-value tasks. If you're serious about working deeply, you need to drain the shallows, you need to schedule time for deep work and spend as little time as possible on shallow work.

By blocking out some time in your working week to perform deeper work, you create greater levels of focus and clarity on what is important in your life. Whatever the work you do, it also allows time to work on YOU, what's important to your wellbeing, relationships and self-reflection; and if you can pull away from your business, work or the activities that you do regularly, this time becomes valuable in working on your life and moving forward with greater levels of clarity, momentum and strength in your conviction.

Rest routines

Having a solid routine that supports a productive rest period, that will allow maximum returns to all aspects of your body, mind and soul, is important to your overall health. Taking a holiday can be beneficial during a scheduled working calendar year, but you don't wish to arrive at your destination exhausted or in a fatigued mode in which you don't enjoy the experiences of the holiday with the richness they deserve.

Firstly, if you regularly listen to your body, mind and aspects of your overall state of emotion, you can quickly adjust aspects of your life that will give you the right level of pick-up you need. When you are always in the 'doing' of life and in the high-performance state, it can be hard to truly slow down. Jumping off the treadmill can often lead to a crash or seeking external distractions such as alcohol.

Light morning and evening walks with a 24 to 48-hour detox from all social media, television and a couple of days on spring water and green tea with light healthy meals will allow you to recharge. Schedule a couple of nature walks, and rev-up with more time meditating, to greatly assist and recharge your productively levels. If you maintain this practice regularly every three weeks during your working schedule, come the end of the year, you arrive in an overall better state of wellbeing.

A golden rule: we have a culture of booze and the national identity is that we seem to think drinking alcohol is associated with a good rest routine. I don't think this is a good example to model to our young generation. Advertising and the booze culture leading up to public holidays needs to have other alternatives.

The PUBLIC HOLIDAY trend is to consume unhealthy levels of alcohol; you have a guilt feeling if you haven't been drinking on a public holiday - you're not an Aussie or you haven't been resting or celebrating life. Endeavour to schedule a reduction of alcohol intake throughout the year, including your work holiday break and on public holidays.

Alcohol should be used for enjoyment and appreciation, like all aspects of our life. The great Australian understanding that a hard-earned thirst at the end of the day should be met with a beer, and the association of drinking with sport, is an unhealthy mindset. It is an Aussie image that needs a rethink, particularly for our young men.

Showing Up - Ups and Downs

When we have the capacity to feel the hard things and truly connect with all parts of our self, it can be a challenging aspect of life but also a necessary one. The shadow also appears when we have truly rested; we are given the strength to deal with these parts of our whole that don't serve us anymore.

Checking out sometimes is okay; it allows us the space to process what is and isn't working for us. We need to ensure, though, that we do not succumb to this habit and the life choice that we describe as 'checking out' from the tough emotions, and only show up for the joyous moments. We don't get to preferentially check out for anxiety, fear or sadness, while checking in for love, joy and excitement. Social media doesn't help with this. Facebook tends to only show the happy moments. It takes a brave soul to be vulnerable and share the low moments in life that we all have.

When we shy away from the big feelings, we shy away from our power and motivation to make change in the world we wish to see. It is a moment of uplifting in our spirit when those big feelings swell up in us and we take the opportunity for greater levels of growth, resilience and deepening of our intrinsic motivation to make the change within us.

Rather than reach for the distraction and/or addiction - be it alcohol, light entertainment on television or perhaps other dark parts of the self - seek greater meaning with this feeling and focus on what you wish to see changing inside you. When in the deep rest state, you have the capacity to dig deep in transforming deep wounds and embracing deeper healing.

High Performance

In his book *High Performance Habits* (2017), Brendon Burchard talks about allowing us to accomplish tasks and work volume beyond the impossible.

> People are tremendously uncertain about how to get ahead with which decisions are right for them, their families, and their careers.

For too many, there is a sense of that things will never get better and they'll always be swimming in a turbulent sea. The surf will always be rolling up a storm - this Is Mother Nature at its best. But in these uncertain times, how we navigate the storm in our ocean, seeking the right habits to provide us direction in a forward high-performance state, is crucial.

High performance can be seen as seeing what's important for us to navigate the sailing boat quickly in the direction we desire. In an emergency or a situation that requires quick action, we may be in a dangerous situation. How we respond to what is important, with quick, powerful decisions, will make us or break us. At the core, I see myself as a lifesaver and lifeguard at sea to rescue someone, in this situation we always consider 'danger to self first'. We need to assess the risk to self before deciding how to respond. Decisions that are made fast and on good trust of self can provide transformation outcomes (managing the risk as best we can) and propel us in the direction we require for change.

The world has changed over the past two years and the state of wait-and-see is never too far from people's horizons. Yet we value planning ahead with a desired vision for everyone, and knowing when we need to be in fifth gear for change is now. Everyone is leading and starting to express truth, yet unsure which direction to take. We see some leaders listening to a collective message about a future we don't all want. How do we forge ahead, with all this traffic and noise causing massive overwhelm? Yet for some it is so easy to go back to bed or drink wine and just switch off from all this negative noise.

> " Not all habits are created equal.
> **Brendan Burchard**

'Burchard' crunches it down to which habits matter most and how you can set up practices that strengthen and sustain them so you move forward with what matters most. We have good, bad and better habits, and some that outshine all the others and help you realise your full potential in your life, relationships and career. Burchard beautifully describes habits that move the needle most in helping you reach high performance when it is critically needed, and habits that ensure you reach all important parts of your life. This includes habits for tactfully getting ahead, and strategic habits for enjoying life.

The term 'high performance' refers to succeeding beyond standards and norms consistently over the long term. It also includes having the ability to master other parts of life, such as nutrition, leadership, self-discipline, relationships, building your own business, and consistently sustaining this pace and space.

We have a popular belief that we should lean into our strengths, and for many years, community development principles has often approached this philosophy within our schools, work places and across community. What if we believed the need to develop people to become whole? We have many examples of people becoming successful in one part of their life, such as a business or professional athletics, but not succeeding in intimate relationships or health.

A high performer shouldn't be frowned upon in our Australian society. Brendan Burchard talks about high performers as being more successful than their peers. I would argue that it depends on how we describe success for some. I have been a 'high performer' at the expense of other parts of my life, but as described in Brendan's book, we can develop the life habits that ensure we perform in all areas of life.

High performers love challenges or a battle to fight; as John Eldredge in his book *Wild at Heart* puts it, the most dangerous man on earth is the man who has reckoned with his own death:

All men die, few men every really live.

The essence of a man's soul is courage and an awakened heart; to express the heart through courage will make the world a better place. High performers are confident that they will achieve their goals despite adversity. Many people are content and relaxed, perhaps grateful with their current situation, whereas high performers believe they will figure things out. They don't shrink from challenge; rather, it helps them progress with what needs to be dealt with and leads them through the turbulence of murky waters that lie ahead.

To see that high performance in all areas of life, we need only adopt the simple philosophy that all aspects of our life are sacred. Life is sacred, and life should be lived wisely. First Nations people understood this concept deeply. Ancient Australia is built on sacred ceremony. The ground we walk on today is sacred. I recall a special event many years ago, when seven monks walked onto Warriparinga for a cultural ceremony with Kaurna Nation cultural Elders. The monks were eternally grateful that their feet were allowed to grace the land that has been worshipped for thousands and thousands of years. It brought tears to my eyes, and a swelling of emotion to understand this concept. Many inspiring leaders that have visited Australia have kissed the earth upon arrival in gratitude. This ancient culture, land and people has been taken for granted and not truly recognised for its global significance.

When high performance is aligned with a deep rest/work pattern, it can lead to increased levels of happiness, health, and growing into abundance in one's life. The other parts of life shouldn't suffer or be lesser. We are not promoting over-consumption, but high performers produce more of what is necessary for sustainable change in self. Having a productive mindset, and doing the things that matter most with greater quality outcomes, will get you to your destination faster.

Focus and effort not only create output that is meaningful for self and the people with whom you connect, but more importantly, they inspire the larger community in the evolving universe that is changing, so that we can keep up with its pace and the rhythmic beat of our Mother Earth.

A closer look at habits, particularly associated with personal growth that moves us towards a desired outcome, is surely good for self and for the people in our life, especially if it leads us to a regular emotional state of consistent connection and comfortable self-actualisation in a safe space. Life throws some of us into complex and challenging circumstances that require us to be high performers. Performing at our best is not something we truly desire, but to be at our best all the time requires some structure, and healthy habits that serve us well. If life throws us a curve ball, we are better equipped to respond and to protect our core and character if we have wellbeing as part of our core, and have developed healthy habits.

I have often been labelled as a high performer in certain aspects of my life. I think the Australian work force is seen as high-performing when we compare ourselves to the rest of the world. In Australia in 2021, the average work week for full-time employees in Australia was 41.8 hours and about 13% of Australian employees worked over 50 hours per week, which is very high. People in OECD countries tend to work longer hours and their values are driven by economic benchmarks set by government policy. Performance, however, isn't about working longer or harder; high performance is having the ability to know when to go into 6th gear, to perform with high quality standards, and then to know what doesn't serve so we can have quality rest or enjoy other aspects of life. This is the high performance and deep work-rest principle. Brendon Burchard simply says: 'to succeed, always remember that the main thing is to keep the main thing the main thing'.

Life throws so much stuff at us, and the human brain can process 11 million bits of information every second. But our conscious mind can only handle around 40 to 50 bits of information a second. It is so important to find stillness in our day. In his book *Aware*, Daniel Siegel advocates cultivating awareness and being aware of when it will rise, so you may integrate information to best fit what allows you to 'perform' at your best. Performance shouldn't be seen as being better than your predecessors or even contemporaries; it is just being better than yourself.

The Australian landscape is covered with sporting heroes, and it is competition that allows us to grow. Competition has contributed to new benchmarks being set in our all aspects of our life, business and community. Too often, though, we see habits forming that don't recognise the other areas of life that keep us in check. Sometimes we can be running too fast and we may miss something, an opportunity in another aspect of life. We have personal responsibilities and habits that serve this space, and social habits that serve our contribution in business and community.

Personal Habits to Cultivate

Seek clarity: How do you want your life to play out? Be clear and define what's meaningful to you.

Generate energy: Learn to understand how to cultivate your energy to best serve you. Be clear on your intentions and keep your energy joyful so it brings you optimum health. 'If I keep up this pace, I'll eventually burn out, or probably just die.'

Raise Necessity: Seek clarity on what you need to have in order to serve. Affirm the why, and level up and define who you want on your squad. As Jim Rohn says: 'Without a sense of urgency, desire loses its value.' When we know our 'A-Game' in what's important, we let go of other things that don't serve us. Work can consume us suddenly and we can be doing work that doesn't serve anyone. This is demonstrated by the analogy of a rainbow serpent eating its own head, which is strongly featured in Aboriginal Dreaming stories across Country.

Social Habits to Cultivate

Increase productivity: Increase the outputs that matter most, chart your five best moves and become epic at key skills that matter.

Become curious: When you have momentum and a system works for you, become insanely curious about why it is working so well and perhaps duplicate this thinking in other areas of your life. I believe that when we are more productive, we become more competent.

> 66 You have to master the primary skills needed
> to win in your primary fields of interest.
> **Andrew Carnegie**

Develop Influence. To lead and champion your message is to teach people how to think, challenge people to grow, and role model the way.

> 66 Power is of two kinds: One is obtained by the fear
> of punishment and the other by acts of love.
> **Mahatma Gandhi**

Demonstrate courage: Honour the struggle, share your struggle and vulnerability, stand and speak your truth, and find someone or something to love and fight for. Courage is an act of love that fights for those who fear their oppressors. It's not always a pleasant feeling. In the moment of courage, we prioritise the love we have for another human being over protecting ourselves and our selfish interest. A courageous act is a noble act of service to people that matter most.

Sustaining Performance in All Areas of Your Life

Aim for humility. Keep an eye on any feeling of superiority within your work and life. When you are succeeding beyond others, it's easy to get a big head. Avoid this attitude and way of thinking. All people contribute equally to the fabric of our society.

As in a healthy ecosystem, we have pelicans, and hawks that fly high, and they are each as important as the beautiful little blue wren who lives in the scrub close to the ground, spreading goodness amongst the lower trees and vegetation.

When we fly high in certain areas of life, it is important that we are aware of sinking into dissatisfaction or neglecting other parts of our life, our purpose, or the important habits that have served us well. Don't take your sustained success for granted.

> **"** There are two kinds of pride, both good and bad. Good pride represents our dignity and self-respect. Bad pride is the deadly sin of superiority that reeks of conceit and arrogance.
> **John Maxwell**

Chapter Six

Alignment

Work-Life Alignment: The Key to a Centred Life of Happiness

When we talk about work-life alignment, we seek wholeness in this space, and move towards embracing how we want to feel in both areas, we then begin to move towards greater levels of happiness. The balance and happiness factor seems to reach new levels if we understand the simple concept of business and life working together as one. Today, people are beginning to value lifestyle, wellbeing and doing 'stuff' that matters; those people are 'awake' and conscious to what is really important.

We have come from a place of belief 'in a myth' that has been told in our modern society: the importance of work-life balance. The concept has been drilled into our heads by so-called experts for years now. We have been told to make sure work doesn't take over our life, and that we don't have too much fun. The aim for 'work-life balance' becomes nothing more than a tug-of-war for our time and energy. When we work too much, we feel guilty and tired, and are not investing enough the other things that interest us in life. So, you go on a holiday and get the balance back.

How can we seek more wholeness and greater alignment in all the areas of life that make us whole and happy?

Achieving Work-Life Alignment

Be aware of what you want in your life and then use your work as the platform for creating the desired future you want. Living a meaningful life is directing your energy and being aware of what you value most in a changing universe and society.

What is important to you? What are your values? And what is precious to you? We have only a limited amount of time. In coaching, we talk about the 'Wheel of Life' model that explores many aspects within our life. These can include family, community, adventure, friends, eating healthy food (wellbeing), reading, being creative, business, living in nature, personal growth, fun, regular holidays, and investing in wealth or lifestyle choices so we can manifest this.

Whether you acknowledge it or not, your life is precious. No one knows how much time they have before it runs out. Yet we never take the time to be clear on what matters most to us, and perhaps just accept life for what it is. I challenge this limiting mindset and I look to the concept that we can move our life and society into whatever is needed for the benefit of people and place, as I am sure many would agree.

Our external environment can sometimes impose a limited mindset, and I also challenge this. We have all the technology and capacity to enable people to help themselves and live a life that serves the self, others and our planet. Ask questions. What are the most memorable experiences in your life? Why were they special? What people, places, things or activities are vital sources of energy for you? What sort of people do you admire? Asking empowering questions that honour the goodness in our experiences uplifts the uniqueness that we all have.

Current Situation with Work

Once we are clear on the values that are important to us and we acknowledge the real 'us', we begin to understand whether our work is in alignment with our life, and whether we are working towards our desired future state.

If you feel in your gut that something is missing when you come home or when you're working, and it doesn't flow, or you drag yourself out of bed to commence your work without excitement and fulfilment, you are seeing the signs that somewhere your alignment is not sitting right. Make big and little life changes. Believe in yourself and ignore the self-doubt and fear of being judged by others and the crazy scary world. Believe me, it will be worth it when you embrace them and start to realign.

Start to Realign

Making the decision to realign isn't a quick-fix process. It doesn't happen overnight. There are some solid structures in many aspects of our life. A good start is to be patient, treating your current working arrangements and your field of expertise with thoughtful insight.

How do you leverage parts of your skills so you can embrace those elements in other parts of your life, so they strengthen your overall life direction and end game? Where do you see yourself at the end of the day? This includes thinking about capacity for working full-time and the idea of moving into a slower lane.

Choose to do the things you have identified you want more of, and explore more ways of making them happen, without any misalignment with the other parts of your life that matter. In this process you will uncover things that don't serve you anymore, and letting them go can be sometimes hard. But it can be a wonderful experience to surrender, lightening the load or the things that niggle, that you have really outgrown.

When you truly focus on key aspects of the life you wish to live, and remain focused, after a while the pace of change in your life can be effective and it can happen quickly. Then you will unleash your rich reserve of energy onto the things that really light up your higher self, passion and purpose.

We are seeing more and more people focusing on their own enterprise, and using this experience as a vehicle for creating the lifestyle they want. Whatever your work-life situation is, we all have the same amount of time in the day. You get to choose how you spend that time and what activities, tasks and people you will work with, to enable you to create the work-life alignment you desire. When life is working for you, greater levels of meaning, purpose and happiness are reached.

Moving in the Space of Alignment

When we reach conscious awareness within our life and we love what we do, how do we stay in the high vibrational state and keep doing what we love doing? First, we need to understand why we do what we do.

A successful business or person really nails the 'why' in the work-life alignment. They have a good understanding of themselves and the inner core of their being, acknowledge what they can offer, and grow into the best they can be in this lifetime. Events and experiences shape us. Bringing meaning allows you to grow when we reach wholeness with these experiences, and you then begin to share your wisdom with others. When you share with others, it can be seen as work. Working to help others on the journey of life is being on purpose and truly aligned to what is most suited for you to grow in the fullest version of yourself.

How you stay on track and adjust to an ever-changing universe and the rhythm of planet earth is the most rewarding part of life. The truth is that the planet Earth and the systems, structures and the groups that make up our society will influence your path. It requires strength, courage, tenacity and determination to go against the grain of energy that travels around the globe, and to move towards something different and unique that doesn't quite fit in the mainstream of society but has the opportunity to change the world for the better.

Readjusting Alignment – Against the Flow

There is energy attached to the forward momentum of going against the grain, or the movement of global systems, structures and people in a general direction. The earth rotates and spins energy from west to east, and the magnetic north and south poles pull energy from north to south. If we find an alignment that works for us, we need to juggle the best we can to keep this momentum in our life, to ensure the parts that we love remain in our life for as long as we can.

This means that, to keep moving and stay in the slipstream of life, we seek clarity in all parts of life so we come back to living a wholesome life. What strengthens this clarity or awareness is when we live with intentions. 'Intentional living' is making decisions and changes that will impact our life, and being aware of what emotion or attitude we attach to this decision. Knowing the emotion we attach to a decision, and being clear what the outcomes of this decision, is being aware of our intentions. This change of direction or slight realignment will encompass greater awareness and better equip us to navigate our life-business relationships, and we will be on a steady, consistent course.

Alignment with Earth for Wellbeing

Our body has energy centres, and just as the Earth does, it holds its own frequency. There's a positively charged electrical field surrounding the Earth but the Earth itself carries a negative charge. While not taken seriously in their time, past scientists such as Nikola Tesla studied the frequency of the Earth. In the 1950s, the German physicist W O Schumann, and his students carried out experiments with electromagnetic waves in the atmosphere and the ionosphere. Schumann discovered a natural pulse resonating around the Earth at a frequency of 7.83 Hz, widely known as the Schumann resonance.

Connecting with the Earth's resonance is essential. Not doing so can lead to lowered levels of melatonin, a cancer suppressant and cell-rejuvenating hormone produced in the brain. Electromagnetic pollution can even inhibit our ability to connect with the earth's natural pulse in a physical sense.

Physicist, *Winfried Otto Schumann* talks about the earth as a living being. Earth is starting to vibrate at a frequency we haven't witnessed before. The frequency of the planet has been increasing very quickly throughout the last 10 years, and has almost doubled. The planet's energy is expanding. The Earth is basically talking to us through her vibration.

The real question is, how are we tuning in to these new frequencies? If we don't tune in, pain is generated, and it hurts a lot. It not only hurts your body; your emotions end up all over the place and your mind becomes a wreck. Some collective thinking is suggesting this change in frequencies is contributing to increased levels of depression in our communities.

Maintaining Alignment with the Rhythm of the Earth

It matters because it's like putting a lightbulb into a circuit that carries more electricity than the lightbulb can handle. If we don't adjust the alignment of our nervous systems, our energetic bodies, the Earth's energy will become just too much for us to take. It's necessary for us to align our bodies with the Earth, allowing us to move more comfortably through this physical world as its energy becomes stronger every day.

We've created the misconception that only a select few can be involved with cultivating a more conscious humanity. But we're all going through this process. Many people are suffering, and not just economically. The number of people with depression is huge. This is because there's a disconnect in the area of life linked to love, inspiration and purpose. Our vibrations aren't aligned with our environment anymore. We're living lives that are not connected to nature, and are not in the rhythm of the cycles of nature.

To be living on Earth right now, if we are not aware of the changes underway, embracing gratitude and drawing stronger connections with our authentic selves, our tribes and the people that matter most, we experience pain. As mentioned, depression is on the increase when we are not aligned. If we don't adapt to this frequency or tune into the rhythm of earth, we go into a separatist mindset.

The Earth has a pulse much like we do; energy travels through the ground to a beat and natural rhythm. The energy travels as a vibration and frequency across the Earth's crust. This movement of energy travels through a grid system much like meridians across our body; and just as we have energy centres in parts of our body, the Earth has a similar lay of the land.

First Nations people have understood this concept, and their lore and culture interweave the story of Mother Earth and the sacred song-lines. I have experienced this first-hand, within Yolgnu (Arnhem Land) and Kaurna cultures (Adelaide). Frequency and vibration are 'sound', much like the 'om' of yoga that we practise on our own body during a yoga class. To attune our body to be in alignment gives us many well-being benefits.

What concerns me today is that this beat or frequency is speeding up and our young people and many others are experiencing an unhealthy mind and an emotional state that is out of balance (for example, depression). The digital economy and the speed of auditory-digital communication (social media) are particularly placing pressure on young people growing up within the auditory-digital world.

Adaptation of species is an interesting concept. Some species within our ecosystems have become extinct. In Australia, particularly over the last 200 years, we have seen large numbers of marsupials disappear due to the impact of our imposed culture and agriculture practices and changes to the landscape through inappropriate land-management practices. First Nations people understand, as natural science confirms, that we are part of the land and form part of the ecosystem.

Some Tips to Ensure You Stay in Alignment with the Earth's Frequency

Increase your fluid intake. Choose filtered water, spring water if you can. Tapping into the minerals from the earth is better for you as it distributes the higher vibration more efficiently throughout your body.

Incorporate more plant-based foods into your daily diet. Plants utilise the natural universal laws of survival, harmonics, mathematics and geometrics, meaning they contain optimum energetic resonance and purpose to survive and thrive.

Step out of the drama of others and bring your focus inward. Investment in other people's stuff only causes you internal chaos because you don't have their resilience resources to solve their challenges.

Be resilient with your own boundaries. Have clarity about where your 'core self' is at.

Get moving. Movement distributes energy around your body. Did you know that movement actually generates kinetic energy in your body to sustain life?

Get yourself into nature more often. Get the shoes off, connecting with the Earth's heartbeat through your bare feet. Connection to nature also stimulates your visual and auditory senses, and supports diffusion of a heightened sympathetic nervous system.

Bring Mother Earth and nature inside your home. Embrace indoor plants, crystals, minerals, salt lamps, and high-quality essential oils - all excellent examples of re-establishing your connection back to nature.

Burn incense with windows and doors open, to encourage regeneration of energy within confined or closed spaces. Clearing your space and claiming it as sacred elevates your energy.

Book regular bodywork such as kinesiology, massage, Bowen and even energy healings such as reiki. Physical manipulation of the body supports flushing of the lymphatic system to enable your body to release toxins and resonate at higher frequencies.

Find slow parts of the day and embrace simplicity. We're moving too fast and can't assimilate the changes in vibration when we're busy.

Live a mindful life and meditate daily. There is clear scientific evidence that meditation alters the brain waves to a deep place of relaxation, perfect for assimilation. Vibrate from the heart rather than your head space.

Embodiment and Grounding

Grounding, or connecting to the earth, is one of the most powerful practices we can use to remain centred in life. Connecting to the earth corresponds to connecting to who we really are. This provides a more emotionally steady ride in life and helps prevent an up-and-down wave.

Simply go outside and with bare feet, stand and spread your feet wider than your hips, at a 45-degree angle, and bend your legs. This will open your hips, and you'll also get to use the strong muscles of your legs to support yourself. Breathe down and into your hips and into your abdomen. Get lost in the sensations that arise.

When we're grounded within our bodies, it becomes easier to receive the imperfect parts of ourselves with kindness rather than with panic or resentment. It might take time to get there, but it's beautiful and worthwhile work.

Source; David Walters www.mindfulword.org

Sound Alignment and Healing

The important parts of the human body's vibration frequency are generally located in about 3 Hz-17 Hz. According to the International Standard ISO 2631, in the vertical vibration of the human body the sensitive range is located in 6 Hz-8 Hz.

Sound is the fastest way to change our vibrational frequency, because with the help of air, we can generate a sound that induces our body, tissues and cells to vibrate. This is one of the reasons why sound healing is so powerful. Sound gets to our core without any trouble, and reaches not only the physical body, but also the energetic body. With the vibration of the sound, we're exposed to, our bodies are able to effectively go back to their natural state of peace, harmony, clarity, intuition and joy.

Whilst working in First Nation communities and experiencing the energy of anger and trauma across the country and downloading the wisdom from the song-lines, I began to feel the sadness which takes a toll on one's health. I can only imagine what this impact is doing to First Nation cultural bearers on their health and how they feel the hurt and damage to country. The healing journey that I initially took was discovering kirtan music within the yoga community. Kirtan is an ancient Vedic tradition of people coming together to sing with a call-and-response style of chanting uplifting mantras, expressing loving devotion to a deity.

Yin Yoga and Songlines

Yin yoga has evolved as a new form of yoga embracing the feminine of the yin-yang Chinese philosophy. *Yin* is the Chinese description of feminine energy. Yin yoga incorporates the *asana* knowledge of traditional yoga, embracing elements of slow-paced exercises, and principles of traditional Chinese medicine. It is an interesting modality when we talk about songlines and energy grids on the earth, and the science of Chinese meridian points across the body, which are sometimes called acupuncture pressure points. Releasing unhelpful energy in the body that needs to be released, yin yoga is a helpful tool in healing and bringing back the flow of energy. The Earth has to release blocked energy through the songlines or grids of energy that flow across the planet, and so we begin to ask how do we release this energy some way? Our First Nations song-men played a sacred and important role in ensuring that song on Country flowed, so healing across Country was always moving.

Humans are always inspired to expand with the evolving universe. We have to embrace this concept so we may grow and evolve our consciousness. Pure consciousness remains infinite and dynamically unchanging, even as it appears as limitless forms and phenomena.

Tat tvam asi (Sanskrit Hinduism) means 'thou art that' and refers to the relationship between the individual and the absolute. How do we do this as a collective so we leave no-one behind? This is where good, sound leadership comes in, to ensure the 'spirit level' is equal for humanity, and always leaning towards alignment. Perhaps this is where politics is at play!

Seasonal Living

Living seasonally is easy. You can start by observing what happens during each season within the natural environment. By observing the weather patterns, tuning into the moon cycles and tide times, and closely observing subtle changes to the patterns during the change of seasons, you will ultimately begin to tune in to yourself. Simple things you could do to welcome the arrival of the seasons would be to visit a community festival, go to a farmers' market, or take a day of rest where you could tune into the change in weather. By spending time outside in nature, feeling the fresh air, being amongst trees, listening to the birds and having ground under your feet, we begin to feel we are part of something bigger.

Patriarchal-Matriarchal Systems at Play with Our Core Alignment

Structurally, we have a stronger patriarchal system at play within Australia and across the world. It is not just in gender-based fields that we need to explore, but when we unpack the patriarchal, it is the masculine energy attached to this system that we should be concerned with. When we have too much *yang* in our body, or the energy systems within us, we develop health issues and our body tells us we need to slow down. This is just as much at play in global politics, economic wellbeing, and across our planet, particularly in the energy grid system and climate change.

Octavia Raheem is an African-American woman who is 'cultivating community through yoga' and calls for a slower pace to life through yoga. In her book *Pause Rest Be,* she explores and inspires the depth of stillness, inviting all of us to resist fiercely, to slow down, let go and listen more. If you are in the midst of vast uncertainty, or are beginning a new life chapter, this book will support you to soften, feel, rest and move closer to the truth of who you are.

The power of men embracing more of the *yin* to restore the sacred balance was first unpacked by award-winning author, academic and environmental activist David Suzuki in his book *The Sacred Balance*. It discusses taking the *yin* and restoring the softness into the fast pace of 'masculine in business', yet still keeping our economy ticking along so we have healthy employment levels, a diverse economy and a healthy workplace. Men have traditionally been taught to provide, and to go forth and strive to achieve in the external world.

Too often I see men at the age of 65, overweight and with health issues, often with a big stomach; this in turn impacts their mental wellbeing with some developing diabetes, and they are unable to find the enthusiasm to enjoy retirement at the fullest. They have worked all their life, and now some reach the concept of retirement with a struggle to adjust from the fast lane into the slow lane of life. The matriarchal system provides this environment and highly values this structure and governance model, so we feel safe to work and play out our life until we can no longer keep up with this pace.

I recall a story told to me once by an Aboriginal man who is a good friend. It involved a rich tourist arriving in Australia on holiday and staying in a five-star resort. The tourist saw an Aboriginal man sitting under a palm tree.

The tourist went over and sat next to the Aboriginal man and said, 'How you going? Do you want to work with me?'

The Aboriginal man said, 'Why do I want to do this?'

The tourist said, 'So you can work really hard.'

The Aboriginal man said, 'Why would I want to do that?'

The tourist said, 'So you can save some money.'

The Aboriginal man said, 'Why would I want to do that?'

The tourist said, 'So you can go on holidays and sit under palm trees and enjoy the sunset.'

The Aboriginal man said, 'That sounds great.'

How do we live on Country and work smarter and not harder? By cutting out all the stuff that we don't need and having strong boundaries so our 'self' remains strong yet soft, and the masculine energy can feel a little of the feminine energy and be okay with this style of living. Sometimes the rituals, routines and structures we have been utilising for a long while take control of our life and suddenly at the age of 60, we find we have missed out on other parts of life. More importantly, when this is done on a collective - a national or global system that is always in 6th gear - we erode not only one life, but future generations.

Another Aboriginal man shared this analogy: it's like a snowball rolling down the mountain getting bigger and bigger and bigger until the snowball is so big when it reaches the bottom of the hill, it's going to crash and do some damage. Another way to look at this perspective is when we are on the treadmill at the gym and we pick up the speed, and it gets faster and faster. We are so in the moment of the drive, determination and passion to keep the speed as we burn calories and feel the blood running through our body, we don't want to stop. It almost becomes a little hard to stop as the rush of hormones and adrenaline has kicked in. Sometimes it's so fast we have trouble getting off.

Perhaps we see some men glorifying the concept of being busy; for them, this fast lane of work life is a strong identity part of self, and it is a struggle to break away from ego, masculine, power-centred life. Stepping away is a new feeling; it is a new identity and can feel a little uncomfortable and uncertain, and creates challenges for some new values that haven't been important in the past. Quite often this is triggered by a health emergency or issue.

Duality (Yara)

I am reminded once again of a lunch meeting when Kaurna Elder Uncle Lewis O'Brien was sharing his wisdom in his indigenous language. Uncle Lewis spoke of the use of duality within all concepts that sustain, and said all things that lead to equality take us forward with more balance and bring us to our true purpose. This is what the word *pa* (*Bar*) means - everything needs to be seen, felt and heard as *equal*; if we see or hear something that is not, we pause and seek greater clarity until we begin to experience clarity. Slowing down needs to be valued for a successful, caring and sustainable society.

Moment of Truth

The golden rule for when we feel things are not quite right and we are out of balance with a task or a part of life that isn't quite right is: pause find the centre and core of 'self' (much like the core of a problem or the core of our Mother Earth) and allow yourself to be present. Being truly present to our situation and listening to our breath is a golden moment. This is the man or the masculine embracing the feminine moment. When this happens, we allow our feelings and emotions to softly come to the surface, bringing a little masculine energy with the feminine energy, and we reach a personal resolve. We ask, 'What are we going to do with this piece of wisdom?' And we move forward in life more whole, and in a centred state of love and joy.

In the same way, when we experience overwhelm in the work place, we are about to experience something new, or we have stepped out of balance with being present with our work or lost in the flow, we just need to take a step back and be okay in the silence.

I am always inspired by the Dalai Lama. When he is surrounded by world leaders, politicians and big business leaders with so much power, he holds his energy to be balanced, always with a beautiful smile and wonderful, wise sense of humour. We should all aspire to leading a life with grace and a good sense of humour as we move forward.

❝ When you live in surrender, something comes through you into the world of duality that is not of this world.
Eckhart Tolle

Chapter Seven

Simplicity

" Simple living is skillful living.
Satish Kumar

O ne of my favorite authors is Satish Kumar. I was most grateful to meet Satish when he came to Adelaide to launch his book *Elegant Simplicity; The Art of Living Well*. Satish suggests we focus on simplicity of mind, thought, speech, feeling, action, food, clothes, house, intention and relationships. Life is a journey as much as a pilgrimage. It is a lifelong process with no final destination. When we seek a true meaning for pilgrimage, we find it is to live free from any attachments, habits or prejudices. Satish talks about pilgrimage as a metaphor as much as a literal reality.

" This grand vision may sound overly idealist, yes perhaps so, but what have the realists achieved? Wars, poverty, climate change? The realists have ruled the world for far too long.
Satish Kumar

According to Satish, an essential ingredient of elegant simplicity is the art of making. We need to move away from automation, industrialization and robotic systems. We need to embrace the idea of mindful making. In First Nations cultures, art is neither a hobby nor a luxury, but rather an essential ingredient of everyday living and being.

Satish was the first to characterise this shift of 'ego to eco'. If we do not wish to complicate our lives, he writes, then we have to shift. Ego separates and eco connects. Ego complicates, eco simplifies. Eco means home where relationships are nurtured.

In another beautiful summary of life, Satish talks about three areas of existence: soil, soul and society, representing the ecological, cognitive and social dimensions of life. Soil is a metaphor for all environmental and natural relationships. Everything comes from the soil. Our bodies come from the soil and they return to the soil. We need to value soil; similarly, we need to replenish and heal the soul. Meditation is one technique for doing this. The wellbeing of soil and soul (the self) must extend to the community or society. The wellbeing of our society is only possible when we organise our communities on the principles of human dignity, equality and social justice.

My father and mother instilled in me this 'decent' value and it has endured within my outlook on life. A decent person is respectable, modest, proper, or fair and kind. I have kept this simple value as I have moved through my life. However, on some occasions when I did not have strong boundaries, and was working in certain tribal sub-culture groups, our kindness can be taken as a given or taken away. When our kindness is stripped away our self-love is taken also. It is how we rise above this tribal culture that values shame and blame and people not respecting people and place that strengthens our character and what we stand for in life. A simple life that values kindness and gratitude for people and place.

In the 19th century, in his book *'Tis a Gift to be Simple*, Joseph Brackett wrote about songs, dances and rituals of the American Shakers. The Shaker song *Simple Gifts* was written in 1848 by Elder Joseph Brackett. Shakers are the supreme example of elegant simplicity, the embodiment of beauty in simplicity. For the Shakers, minimalism is a way of life.

> 66 'Tis the gift to be simple.
> 'Tis the gift to be free.
> **Shaker folk song *Simple Gifts***
> **written and composed in 1848**
> **by Joseph Brackett**

Gandhi was another great champion of simplicity in life. 'Simple living and high thinking' was his motto. Gandhi lived in a simple hut which he had built himself, spun the yarn for his loin cloth, grew vegetables and cooked his own food, while leading the Independence Movement of India and editing a weekly journal.

Simplicity focuses on the quality of life rather than the quantity of material possessions. It is about being rather than having. Eric Fromm puts it this way: 'When I live a life of simplicity, I celebrate the intrinsic value of making and letting go of focusing on results or outcomes, achievements or accomplishments.'

Simple living is its own reward. It is also skillful living – learning not only to use our heads and hands, but also to cultivate our heart qualities of love, forgiveness, and the understanding of the unity of all life.

> 66 Simplicity, patience and compassion
> are our greatest treasures.
> **Lao Tzu**

Cultivating equanimity in our hearts as we navigate our way through life's challenges allows us to see the world as whole and not to get caught up in the duality of good and bad, pain vs pleasure, gain vs loss.

One of my favorite passages that *Satish Kumar* wrote 'elegant simplicity is as good for the outer landscape of the ecosphere as it is good for the inner landscape of the soul. The way to sustainability is simplicity. Simplifying our homes, our workplaces, and our lives is the way to create a sustainable world for our children.'

There is an outer and an inner journey of simplicity. We can live a life of environmental stability, spiritual fulfilment, and social justice. We can live with calmness and composure, especially in a difficult situation. This inner journey of equanimity builds peace within and then we project this peace outwards to others.

> " Simplicity is the ultimate sophistication.
> **Leonardo Da Vinci**

Living a simple life is being engaged in making and doing, thinking and feeling. In all these activities, we need to cultivate simplicity. How can we be simple while cooking with family, gardening, taking a shower, or cleaning the house? By doing every action, from large to small, with a light touch, a small footprint. The moment we make things heavy, life becomes complicated. In living a simple life, we flow through life as a river traverse through the country.

Complexity is not the same as complication. Complexity is natural and beautiful. Simplicity and complexity are complementary. Our bodies are very complex. The microorganisms and bacteria in our bodies are complex. Yet the body is also very simple. We all manage our bodies quite well. We eat, we shower, we wash, we go to the toilet, and we sleep; we do everything in a simple way and manage our beautiful complex body and its structure.

Existence is complex, yet simple. Academics and economists make it complicated. Living a simple life is rooted in consciousness, which means 'knowing together'. Consciousness connects us with the past, present and future, with our ancestors and future generations, with time and space, with matter and spirit. Consciousness is the ground of our elegantly simple relationship with the universe. The universe and all our actions within it emerge out of consciousness. Sun, moon, stars, planets, galaxies, trees, oceans, mountains and humans are all manifestations of consciousness. Consciousness is the ultimate reality.

The intimate human mind is linked to the ultimate universal mind. From ultimate to intimate we have no gap and disconnect; it is whole and beautiful. To live a wholistic life is to flow with grace and pure love aligned to consciousness. With this cosmic reality, there is an implicit order. What looks like chaos is in fact orderly. This order maintains abundant life forms. It has wonderful simplicity.

Out of our fear of chaos, we have developed complicated systems. Our lives are now controlled by the clock, the diary, meetings and a lot of structure. The Australian outback appears wild, harsh and foreign, but there is order, self-management and self-maintenance. Nature takes care and it is orderly and in flow. The life of the mother and the life of mother nature resemble each other. To practise living simply requires practice of spontaneity and improvisation.

> 66 Life is a pilgrimage; Faith is not the clinging to a shrine but an endless pilgrimage of the heart.
> **Abraham Joshua Heschel**

If someone comes to your door unexpectedly, do you invite them in? The word for 'guest' in the Indian tradition is *atithi*, which means one who comes without appointment. In every situation we need to allow for the unplanned, the unexpected event, we need to be flexible and spontaneous. New things are always emerging. Embrace the emergent situations and welcome this flowing with nature.

If we have excessive planning and the plan doesn't work out, we will be disappointed. Instead of planning, let us have vision. A vision is like a dream state. Cultivating a dream state allows the future to evolve and emerge as it will. When we plan too much in advance, opportunities may be blocked. When we know enough is enough, we have more than enough.

Simplicity offers sufficiency over extravagance, comfort over convenience, contentment over cravings, reconciliation over resentment at Satish Kumar provides insights into the Art of Living Simply. It means sincerity and honesty within as well as the reduction of clutter. It means restraining oneself in one direction and allowing other areas in your life to flourish with abundance. It means music, gardening, family, time for friends, new hobbies, and avoiding mass production and mass consumption.

> **"** I have just three things to teach: simplicity, patience and compassion. These three are your greatest treasures.
> **Lao Tzu**

To Raise Conscious, Caring Children

What really matters most to families is leaving a legacy for our children, and how I play a role in shaping their view on the world, to be caring people that contribute to community for the next generation. I have always been inspired by cultures and families that value inter-generational upbringing. I am grateful for my parents and their contribution in bringing up my two beautiful children. First Nation cultures highly valued inter-generational wisdom, and Elders, Uncles and Aunties contributed to bringing up all the children in the community. We must believe that every child deserves to be educated and raised with an appreciation for how life works, and to be grounded and see the truth of living well.

The Danish School of Thought

Denmark has been voted one of the happiest countries in the world over an extended number of years. Life is simple when we understand how we pass on some important values to the next generation, our children. Danish parents raise happy children who grow up to be happy adults who raise happy children, and the cycle repeats itself.

They focus on how they nurture the little self and embrace a concept called *hygge* (pronounced 'hoo-ga'). This Danish lifestyle and parenting concept is about being 'cosy', especially with those we love. It literally means 'to cosy around together'. This reminds me of the way Eskimo people snuggle together with their family. Instead of an authoritarian parenting style ('You'd better do that right now!'), the Danish approach sidesteps power struggles and works toward maintaining respect. Danish parents explain the rules and give their children warmth and trust.

Parenting Danish Style

Let your children play, and in particular let your children play freely. Encourage them to play outside in nature and explore with other children of different ages. Child-led play builds self-esteem. Let your children explore to see what comes naturally.

Be honest with your children. Tell your children what you really think, good and bad.

Promote further discussion by asking why they like or dislike things, to enable their own self-discovery journey.

Choose good books to read, with good values and honest conversations. Importantly, read together as a family.

Embrace togetherness and the Danish concept of *hygge*, a time of cosiness with friends and family. Playing a family game or sharing stories builds connection and values a sense of belonging.

If a negative situation arises, take the time to discuss the issue; 'reframe' it with the child and see it for what it is, not to rose-colour the issue but to help your child focus on what they can do rather than what they can't.

Don't give ultimatums, but rather, be clear with setting rules and boundaries, and avoid the authoritarian style of parenting which takes away respect and erodes trust. If the child is upset, guide them through the emotions and when they reach a calm state it's much easier to talk.

Practise empathy. We want to raise children who show compassion for themselves and for others. This is about teaching children to understand people. A good way to practise empathy is to talk about facial expressions and the range of feelings that they reflect.

Let the child work it out. Often parents try and step in when a child is playing with other children and a problem may arise that may upset their child. When you feel the need to step in, take a step back and see if the children can find a way to negotiate and learn some skills in resolving the conflict themselves.

Source *The Danish Way of Parenting*, Jessica Joel Alexander and Iben Sandahl

Seeds of Inspiration

The 'Seeds of Inspiration' program in Canada is a wonderful initiative which began with one idea in mind: the simplest learning experience can inspire children for a lifetime. The wonder of planting a seed and seeing it grow into a thriving plant gives children a sense of pride, accomplishment and a feeling of their importance on planet Earth.

" A child is like a seed. With the right conditions, the seed has the potential to become that which is inside a beautiful strong tree, plant or flower that blossoms and shines for all to see.
'Plant a seed and see what grows Foundation'
https://seewhatgrows.org/about-us/

Chapter Eight

Forager Landscapes and Natural Cycles

Groundwater

An ancient land that has endured millions of natural cycles across the oldest contingent of land 'Gondwana' on planet earth and the oldest surviving culture on planet earth. Gondwana land 'Australia' is sacred land, yet today we see a future of change in land-economics, if we dare to choose the right path for people and place.

How we live on Country is the basis of a future for generations to come. To live well and embrace all the resources that Mother Nature provides is to be grateful. As we move forward into a new world, having an abundant mindset that community embraces will offer us an opportunity to reconnect to nature once again.

Australia has a fascinating underground flow of water storage systems leading into the Great Artesian Basin. It is the largest and deepest artesian basin in the world, stretching over 1,700,000 square kilometers, with measured water temperatures ranging from 30-1000C. The basin provides the only source of fresh water through much of inland Australia.

Many of the Dreaming stories of First Nations people talk about springs and teach the wisdom of how to live on Country based around water. They also include other key features of landscape and ecology. Australia has the oldest surviving literature of song-lines across Country and it is a fascinating view of how the Earth works. The wisdom that this thinking teaches is not to be underestimated. It is important for all people.

First Nations people have already endured climate change. Archaeological evidence clearly indicates that Aboriginal people have experienced glacial and inter-glacial periods throughout their history. Climate change is real and we are on the brink of a big climate emergency never witnessed before in humanity's evolved consciousness. Our underground water should be seen as a social asset for all Australians. Water and food sovereignty should be at the forefront of social capital, and policy development should ensure all Australians live equally on Country.

Why did the first Nations people introduce fire farming on this ancient land? There are many benefits to 'thinning' the landscape to ensure wildfires do not harm our communities, as we have seen today. With the onset of climate change, we will see far greater wildfires if the future, if we are unable to control it. Wildfires today pose one of the biggest problems on Country, especially with the encroaching challenge of climate change.

The new Australians are still newcomers to this land. There is increasing knowledge and evidence of fire's use as the ultimate management of land within Australia. It is undebatable that First Nation people of Australia were the oldest sustainable farmers on Earth. They uniquely understood their environment and how to manage it effectively and safely for biodiversity and survival, and they understood the features of the land mass through the ancient song-lines of Australia.

Peter Andrew's book *Back from the Brink* (2001) highlights some notable facts about Australia's unique water behaviour, its flow across high Country and seepage into natural landscapes, and it provides some insights into how agriculture can be improved across the landscape.

To love country and appreciate the subtleness of soils and vegetation is understanding Australia. Charles Massy book - *Call of the Reed Warbler* talks about the uniqueness of the fragile landscapes and grasslands across Australia. I see First Nations cultural song-men love country so country will love them back, country speaks and if we listen to country, it will love us back with wisdom and guide us through the seasons.

Environmental historian *Cameron Muir* provided deeper insights 'there is a dimension of war about the way Australians colonial have approached their land, understanding it as mongrel country, rather than a functioning ecosystem poorly adapted to the expectations of western agriculture.'

I question the concept of *terra nullius* that was defeated by Eddy Mabo in the High Court of Australia. Seven judges found that the Meriam people were 'entitled as against the whole world to possession, occupation, use and enjoyment of the lands of the Murray Islands'. This High Court judgement set as record and truth that Australia was settled before the arrival of Captain Cook. I now begin to question our current Government's lapsing into the concept of *terra nullius* ('nobody's land'), and not caring for country or fire-proofing or managing our agriculture and water use for the future. We see good people sharing this wisdom, but an overall lack of action on the part of mainstream Australia.

Today we are beginning to see less interest in large-scale mining as the world embraces renewable energy sources. In the past, we have traditionally been seen as the quarry of the world, and in the previous century, the food bowl of the world. The landscape is changing and we need to truly embrace our age. It's time for Australia to grow up, embrace the wisdom of this Great Southern Land, and stand up for what is right.

I see a change in 'land economics'. Never before have we been in a position to live on Country in an ecologically sustainable way, and move into supporting the 17 goals identified in the United Nations Sustainable Development Goals. We have the technology and innovation available within the fields of sustainable technology at local, regional and international levels. It is now about helping the people and communities to transition to this new way to live on Country.

I recall listening to a conversation with an Aboriginal Elder some 20 years ago. She was about why we have a food system that has been developed on Country with the philosophy of the city and the farmer. She was curious about why we all live in the city and all the farms that grow our food are all located out in the country some 500kms or more away.

Natural Food Systems

The concept of food miles is interesting. The idea of low food miles has become marketable and is a social trend across regional food bowl communities around the world. Numerous bio-regions and communities embrace farmers' markets, encouraging communities to buy direct from the farmer, and this is proving to be most beneficial in achieving sustainable objectives.

My home town and bio-region of the Southern Vales, south of Adelaide on the Fleurieu Peninsula, has the first farmers market to be established in South Australia: The Willunga Farmers' Market. I was grateful to work for this great South Australian icon. 'Willunga' (*willangga*) is a Kaurna name for the locality of green trees.

It has always been a challenge to create a healthy environment for ethical farmers to embrace 'best practice' in growing clean and green fruit and vegetables. I have spoken to many good Farmers that take their produce to 'markets' and embrace good standards, but we are yet to see the big supermarkets actively supporting farmers. 'Truth on labelling' on products we buy from the big supermarkets, particularly fruit and vegetables, is a challenge which may help support farmers to do the right thing by growing the best produce sold in our food stores and supporting our ecosystems. We need to educate mainstream Australia to embracing this way of life. Food is our medicine and the seeds on country will bring us home for the better of people and place.

This is a recognition of the value of diversity in the food system. This system is less reliant on the super food stores and mass production, that attempts to feed the mass population, but a system that sustains a healthier and more sustainable lifestyle. It is a system that values the community's greater connection to fresh food, soils and our natural environment.

Environmental peace activist Satish Kumar talks about 'soil, souls and society' as the basis for sustaining life and living well on planet Earth. When we choose healthy, fresh plant foods that haven't been treated with pesticides, and animals that are cared for by farmers the old ways, we are becoming part of a local ecosystem that is managing the landscape in such a way that it increases the biodiversity of the land. As more and more people are being connected to this system, this is a good story for everyone and should be embraced by everyone.

My father was a chef and dietitian, resourceful in using all parts of animal products and vegetables. Food waste is a significant issue in our hospitality sector, yet this is actually an opportunity for efficiency, if chefs and café owners were to be innovative and creative in their cooking, it would not only add a point of difference. It would be ethical, and a key value the consumer will demand as we begin to recognise that our food system is unsustainable. First Nations people have always respected how they kill an animal for ceremony and consumption, for the greater good of their community and their respective language group. When I witnessed Aboriginal communities consuming all parts of the kangaroo, including the delicate sweet-tasting tail, it reminded me how Dad was always resourceful in the kitchen. Chefs and the hospitality sector need to embrace native foods in their cooking, the nutritional benefits far outstrip the traditional foods we grow. It is also good for country and the natural landscapes.

Accessibility

We should be supporting food systems in which farmers and the agriculture sector all support and increase the biodiversity across a bio-region. It will strengthen local fauna and flora prominent in the region, and enable strong connections between agriculture and of conservation and National Park groups. And hopefully we will see more inclusion and accessibility to the community at large. Too often this space is seen as inaccessible or distant to mainstream Australia. These groups need to broaden their message and continue to take the community on a shared journey of learning. In my home state of South Australia, the Government recently allowed the public to have access to our water reservoirs and water storage dams for recreation use and appreciation of the natural beauty. I feel this is sending the right message to the broader community; respecting our natural resources and accessing them is a strong message that we all belong to the land.

The agriculture sector and farmers need to draw on First Nations wisdom. That includes burning and thinning parcels of land to ensure fire safety, and ongoing cultural practices that complement our climate and soils. Governments need to reduce the red tape that hinders windows of opportunity to back-burn quickly when the right conditions present themselves. The length of time it takes to undertake a 'cultural burn' or 'burn-country' by government authorities can often mean the opportunity may be lost while regulatory approval is sought. As with any new land management practice, it requires practice and building confidence amongst people to ensure we get it right, as we deal with public safety.

Governments and the community alike need to value investing in First Nations knowledge as competent fire keepers. Only then can we begin to see the re-emergence of wisdom in this space, as once again an effective, efficient and wholistic approach to burning vegetation and embraces the old knowledge. Adopting strategies such as burning smaller areas with less intensity means canopies won't be scorched and soil compost will remain intact. This approach of fuel-reduction burning allows firefighters to be safer and more effective on the fire line, and it can protect farms and communities from damage.

I also believe that forest thinning is a good way to accelerate the ecological maturity of old growth forest. It is also the most risk-averse approach, as small trees fighting for light tend to hold less moisture and also become fuel.

In his book *The Biggest Estate on Earth*, Bill Gammage has identified how First Nations people made Australia. He clearly indicates that the landscape was carefully manicured; understanding the unique landscapes allowed for small-scale interventions to slow, spread and sink stormwater along water-courses which ultimately led into the ground. Water in the ground is stored and not evaporated, which is particularly important in a hot climate with high levels of evaporation. Rehydration approaches offer great promise in addressing the drought landscape and bushfire crisis. Creating a chain of ponds and wetland systems, as some Councils have undertaken, should be congratulated, and we should persist with this wetland system.

Salinity

As previously highlighted by a number of experts, Australia has a unique water-course system that has evolved, together with an ancient method of recharging water into aquifers over thousands of years. As described by Gammage, Australia has the largest underground water storage in the world. Our soils are ancient, our vegetation is drought tolerant yet also highly flammable - hard facts to swallow. First Nations people understood the basic rules for ensuring the movement of water across the landscape, and in some notable examples water even defied gravity. Wetlands were considered vital in ensuring water was moving at all times, and in times of drought vegetation coverage across wetlands ensured plants remained alive until the next rain. The Adelaide plains had an extensive pattern of wetlands and moving water systems extending the length of the Adelaide airport and the main coastal strip and coastline.

The Tjilbruke Dreaming story of the Adelaide (kaurna) people talks of Tjilbruke the lore man and fire keeper, who turned himself into the wetland bird, the sacred Ibis. First Nations people understood we must always 'keep an eye' on the wetland water birds to ensure their habitat was healthy. In a large proportion of Australia, including outback communities, the topography of the land was shaped by water courses and wetland landscapes.

If a salinity issue breaks out, it must not be viewed in isolation, but seen in terms of how we embrace modern agriculture practices. It would be important to pump water out of the area of concern whilst still understanding natural topography issues, that is, what is happening to the water and soil conditions. In managing the salinity issue, we must plant native vegetation and good ground cover across Country, whilst appreciating the movement of water across Country and into other storage areas will assist with reducing the salts building up into the soils. Salinity issues involve both soil and water; and in the past as well as today, it is still considered expensive to deal with them. But when we consider the long-term costs of not repairing the build-up of salt in surface soil, in particular dryland areas, is it really expensive? If we choose not to take this action, we will begin to see a die-back of Country and loss of the capacity of the land to provide its richness.

Living on Country in Our Home

It is time for the building industry and consumers to appreciate and value the design of new-build homes. Currently 2% of home builders in Australia engage an architect to custom design a home that fits the location and people's requirements, while also considering the ecological footprint of their home. Today we still see project home designers building homes for profit and not for people. I hear of many building inspectors experiencing an increase in the number of homes requiring significant repairs and maintenance due to poor workman-ship as builders cut corners.

We need to value homes that suit our lifestyle, particularly ecolog-ically sustainable homes that bring the outdoors inside and connect with nature more. We should be zoning homes, as we see with permac-ultures principles. When parts of the outside world come inside, people connect with the consciousness of nature and are drawn into greater connection with their communities. Sadly, too many homes today encourage a disconnect from nature.

Climate-responsive homes allow communities to truly embrace the natural cycles of local climates. Too often homes have wasted space, perhaps because we have been generous with building, keeping our eyes on the big castle concept. I heard this concept called the 'brink venereal disease' and it leads to slap-dash housing development; it does nothing to serve the community, neighbors and a village lifestyle that would encourage greater connection. Even as we witness more people living in isolation and feeling disconnected, and an increase in depression, we build homes with high fences and four walls, that do nothing to nurture connection and encourage the community to come together.

How can we renovate homes so that people can reconnect to nature, adding spaces (and perhaps less space), that are efficient? We need to allow for architecture and design to provide spaces with multiple functions within a home. A bigger home isn't always better. We need to seek out architects and designers who will broaden the scope of how to feel, see, and listen to Country in our homes.

Most Australians have not experienced homes of quality and comfort, in contrast with homes from Europe, North America that are designed for harsh climates. In order to feel at home when we bring the outside in, we shouldn't be afraid to embrace climate-conscious design, so we will feel warm in winter and cool in summer without embracing the aircon. The air conditioner is a band-aid solution to climate management in homes. Climate-responsive design should be the end product of home design. Air-conditioning reliant homes are hungry for power, add to the long-term expense of a home's utility bills and the current carbon system.

A government website – www.yourhome.gov.au - provides some wonderful insights into how to build and design your home to be more environmentally sustainable. Current building standards have a 10-star rating for energy efficiency homes set by the government and building codes/regulations. Not many homes reach the minimum rating of 6 stars out of 10. A recent study by the CSIRO indicated that housing is not meeting these industry standards, with a large proportion of homes only achieving 4.5 rating.

The building 'wrap' or building membrane needs to be incorporated into the home design and build. Often this is left out or installed poorly. The concept of three skins - skin, clothing and then the home as the 'shelter' - is used widely in design for comfortable living. The *wodli* is a Kaurna word for shelter (Aboriginal people of the Adelaide Plains, South Australia). Our *wodli* – shelter designs - don't seem to be taking into account Maslow's hierarchy of needs. With our basic need for shelter, how can we expect humans to live in harmony and as good citizens?

To add to this, the complexity of housing affordability and the competitive rental market mean that urbanised societies are undergoing competing pressures. Eco-development and permaculture, with people embracing sustainable lifestyles, provide real solutions with worthy examples to assist embracing the *wodli* and a sustainable village concept for everyone, including marginalised members of our community, to access.

Current statistics show many homes were built only 30 years ago, and homes being built today will generally have a 30-year life expectancy - a reflection of a throwaway society. This is poor practice and unsustainable for the precious resources being extracted from people (workers) and Country (land).

The Suburbs, City and Vertical Farms

Retro-suburbia, a beautiful book by David Holmgren, explores how Australians can downsize and retrofit a lifestyle that enables a home and garden to be more sustainable and resilient in big cities. It shows projects that are challenging but exciting, and provide more satisfying work and a meaningful way of living. The lifestyle offered aligns to the philosophy of thinking about the next generation as we live in uncertain times.

Mainstreaming Permaculture

Permaculture has often been seen to be inaccessible to mainstream society, with people finding it not only difficult to access but difficult to understand; or perhaps they simply do not feel the need for this lifestyle. Some components of permaculture may come across as too 'hippy' or 'alternative' for the Aussie. An appreciation for living with nature is not felt by a large proportion of the population. However, I see this changing, as we continue to live beyond our means and the ill health of people and place continues to impact communities.

For too long we have lived beyond our means, and pressures are beginning to be felt across the suburbs. The appeal of living in harmony with people that align to our values will continue to build an interest in permaculture communities, especially as they get better in marketing the eco-village lifestyle as a vibrant and attractive alternative to current housing and urban living.

❝ The universe is not a collection of objects
but a communion of subjects.
Thomas Berry

Every being has a fundamental worth; no-one is disposable, and all deserve respect. Social and ecological injustices are rooted in disconnection from the sacredness of all lives, human and otherwise. We must confront planetary shortfalls. This involves restoring a humble appreciation of the sacred part of every living thing. First Nations people understood this sacredness and that every living thing is connected. When we embrace the concept that diversity is the backbone of ecological resilience, we create a life-enhancing society; we must honour universal worth and celebrate various identities. To collectively heal from the systems that divide us, equitable access for those from historically marginalised communities must be a priority.

In our regional and urban communities, there are many examples of permaculture developments where we see communities operating successfully, including some in my home town:

- Troppo architecture business and the Whitmore Square Adelaide city development café (www.troppo.com)
- Sturt Street, Adelaide; Urban Ecology Australia (https://www.urbanecology.org.au/eco-cities/christie-walk/) a notable model for eco-city development.
- Aldinga Arts Eco Village (https://aldingaartsecovillage.com)
- Food Forest, Gawler, South Australia https://foodforest.com.au/about-us/permaculture/

Other notable interstate eco-villages embracing permaculture principles within a village setting are:

- Krishna Village in northeastern New South Wales, (https://krishnavillage-retreat.com/) - although a retreat and yoga centre, the site embraces innovative permaculture and organic garden and sustainable living accommodation

- Crystal Waters located in Conondale, Queensland, https://crystalwaters.org.au/about/.

Land Economics

How can we present eco-developments like the models above as more accessible to mainstream Australia, so people don't feel that this way of living is too much of an alternative lifestyle? Perhaps it requires a softer, more accessible marketing and awareness campaign that takes people on a journey of education and discovery about living more in harmony with nature. The time is now, as economic conditions allow more eco-developments or retro-fit in the suburbs, and we can reach people at all levels of socio-economic circumstances.

People-friendly and community-friendly design of villages and homes can be seen in my home town of Aldinga. The Aldinga Arts Eco Village has no fencing and a village feel to the housing development. Let's design homes that are climate-ready; shading, particularly, is important as a key feature in making homes more comfortable.

The changing face of the land economics model that is taking place, with an increase in living off-grid in smaller homes, will increase the interest and market demand for eco-community-village projects and encourage home owners looking to retro-fit their existing home.

Native Foods to the Landscape and Farms

The concept of foraging doesn't mean collecting wild greens and bush foods. However, encouraging more of our native foods into our food system will help the Australian landscape as people will begin to understand the natural landscapes. The benefit of bringing our native foods into our food-mix and cooking is significant, not only for our landscapes and environment, but for us too. Some of the native foods are considered 'super foods', for example, the Kakadu plum.

Foraging in the urban setting is an attempt to shop for food that isn't meeting ethical standards whilst addressing some basic needs of our biodynamic body. Our body is intrinsically connected to nature, and the rhythm and subtle elements of seasonal change is always felt by the body. So, food that is sourced locally has more health benefits for the human body. Native foods have not been genetically modified and contain high strains of good DNA, and are particularly rich in magnesium, zinc and calcium. Native foods also have higher anti-oxidants levels than our standard introduced crops on Country, particular the mono-culture cropping that dominates our agriculture sector.

Today we see the big supermarkets yet to embrace the concept of 'truth on label' for our fruit and veggies. But how do we encourage the agriculture sector to embrace sustainable farming practices when our agriculture sector is the least subsidised in the world? A large proportion of Australia's soils are mineral deficient, and a significant proportion of our good soils have been developed with housing, industry and cities.

Greening Big Cities

Today we are beginning to see highly populated cities embrace the importance of cooling. Urban planners and governments are encouraging projects to plant more shade and vegetation cover across the built environment, including innovative green wall irrigation systems that support plants growing up tall buildings. Climate change will have a significant impact on high-density environments built mostly of hard building materials that hold the heat.

Dr Brenda Lin, CSIRO Interdisciplinary Ecologist, states urban greening will increase the social, economic and cultural value of our city communities. In the City of Sydney, as in many big cities, space is an issue in introducing greener spaces into an over-crowded urban concrete jungle. Canopy wall mountain coverage and high-density 'pocket forests', developed by Japanese botanist Akira Miyawaki, allow planting and installation of dense forests across Asia and other parts of the world. It is a notable step that has captured a vision and encourages us to imagine that maybe we can green our world.

There is a contrast between visiting and living in big cities and small country towns and outback communities. Too often it becomes a significant contrast for people in cities when they see people living in suburbs and regional country towns; it just doesn't seem possible to tackle the question of how to significantly change our concrete cities and find a direction towards a better world where people will feel connected to nature.

We should value the ability to change our future within urban landscapes across all fields of infrastructure: transport, parks, waterways, vegetation, lakes and rivers within cities. Our central planning agencies should locate greenfield developments that tackle the issue wholistically. Local governments need a strong voice and access to higher levels of infrastructure funding; funding should be based on agreements meeting ecological urban development standards, whilst also aligning to the United Nations 17 goals for sustainable development. To realise a vision of greener cities and change our future urban landscapes, we need to view green infrastructure as more important than traditional infrastructure developments. Green infrastructure needs to be driven by local communities at a local level, not the level of state or national government, at the hands of big developers and multi-nationals. We need to engage in skill transfer to infrastructure consultants and the business sector, driven by consultation with people who live and work in big cities about what will serve them best.

We see infrastructure development undergo rigorous economic assessment and risk assurance processes, which often slow down the development process. They are important; but when doing a cost-benefit analysis, let us be accountable and align the reporting to the United Nations 17 goals on sustainable development and climate change. Time is of the essence and Rome wasn't built in a day. For humans living in big cities, their environment that won't be pleasant moving forward, as a big issues such as climate change, a disengaged workforce, and rising social and economic pressures pose a real challenge.

We may see a movement of people away from big cities and into the regions, as they seek a better lifestyle and a cleaner environment. Over an extended period of time, social planners forecasting this trend would allow the space in big cities for green corridors, and build natural landscapes back into the cities of the world.

City of Adelaide

According to *The Economist* Intelligence Unit's Global Livability Index for 2021, my home city of Adelaide is ranked as the third most livable city in the world, making Adelaide the most liveable city in Australia. In Adelaide, we see the foresight of good planning by the first Surveyor-General of South Australia, Colonel William Light. The city is surrounded by parklands, much like the city of New York, and provides a natural landscape that ensures the CBD is never too far from a green space. Adelaide has all the modern aspects of a sophisticated city, arts culture, including festivals that are often staged within the parklands, creating a vibrant city atmosphere. Importantly, the parklands and modern city design with effective planning has enabled life in Adelaide without congestion and cramped living.

Colonel William Light was guided by a Kaurna man, Mullawirraburka. Let us not forget how first Nations people warmly welcomed migrants and helped shape some parts of their destiny of how to live on Country well. Mullawirraburka, a Kaurna leader, was born in Willunga, where I grew up as a young boy. His name means 'dry forest old man' and he was a skillful leader. I was most fortunate to listen to early stories from Kaurna Elders who have since passed away. They tell of how Mullawirraburka showed aspects of good Country to Colonel William Light and another early settler, George French Angus, who was an English painter, naturalist, poet and explorer. George was the son of George Fife Angus, who was a notable contributor to the establishment of early South Australia.

We have spoken about 'vegetation thinning' and fire management on country, we have spoken about Bill Gammage and Bruce Pascoe's books on how Australia looked before the arrival of the first fleet, the Great Estate in that country was managed and clearings of land was managed for safety. Uncle Lewis O'Brien shared how the Adelaide Parklands shape around the city provide a necessary green corridor of open grasslands much like Australia would have appeared across country. Colonel William Light no doubt formed a positive relation-ship seeking wisdom and knowledge on surveying and planning the City of Adelaide from Kaurna leaders.

Mullawirraburka showed George French parts of the south coast and the southern Peninsula. *French* was then commissioned by the British Government to paint landscapes, capturing Kaurna people in their natural landscape across Country, fishing, hunting and in cere-monial dance. These paintings then became 'postcards' encouraging English people to migrate to South Australia.

This is an example of how a respected Aboriginal leader engaged positively with two prominent leaders during early settlement of South Australia. Considering the mistreatment of so many other Aboriginal people by white settlers, we must always be grateful to First Nations people for being so welcoming to settlers in South Australia.

> **"** Let us develop respect for all living things. Let us try to replace violence and intolerance with understanding and compassion. And love.
> **Jane Goodall**

Chapter Nine

Conscious Living

To Live and Work Well

> " What is true is good. Truth gives us strength
> and allows people to grow into their purpose.
> **Proverb**

To reference a wonderful book titled *Country* written by Bill Gammage and Bruce Pascoe: northern hemisphere people became farmers. Farmers think differently. Their draught horses wear the blinkers that agriculture imposes on them, and this affects how they see Country. Farming means settling down, drawing lines on maps, building fences.

> " Fences on the ground make
> fences in the mind.
> **Bill Gammage**

Australia had not a single fence in 1788, not a single marker that cultivators might recognise as bounding property or claiming ownership. Management of Country was invisible to the invaders; however, the new Australians transformed fire from friend to fiend, and the unconscious irony is that in the making of the new Australia we see today, we have unmanaged the land, *terra nullius*, for the migrants.

Living on Country requires awareness of our uniqueness. We should be looking less to Europe, America and other parts of the globe and their cultures and values, and stop imposing these ideas how we are to live in Australia.

Awareness and intentions have a collective impact on consciousness. Intentions contain more commitment than desires. Intentions are less specific, less rigid, and thus less likely than goals to trigger unhealthy attachments to outcomes. Setting meaningful, effective intentions involves a spiritual as well as a practical, strategic approach to living well.

When we understand that intentions can work for a healthy lifestyle that makes us happier and fulfilled, we are recognising our truth – the truth that our wellbeing is the fundamental part of our existence, necessary to live the best life. The concept of Living Well is understanding how your 'being' is in your life. What are your current circumstances, emotional, physical and spiritual, and how best can you move forward whilst growing your emotional, physical and spiritual wellbeing?

To live consciously is a journey of discovery, in which you embrace and accept the loving nature of 'self' and restore your inner values of love. Living consciously, you are aware of and in touch with the automatic aspects of yourself which debilitate you. You choose new ways of responding to the world you live in and how you express yourself. With this openness, you seek new ways and pathways to express your centred self. You're comfortable enough take care of yourself with greater levels of compassion, self-kindness and patience within your inner world, which are expressed in your outer world, leading to a kinder world.

Too often we overstep some of these parts of our lives. We overdo some exercises and our body hurts the next day; we over-give some of our energy and the level in our emotional bucket drops or behaves in such a way that we miss the point of life and commit a sin or make a mistake, and it impacts on our higher self and how we feel about ourself.

Physical Wellbeing

Physical wellbeing is the ability to maintain a healthy quality of life that allows us to get the most out of our daily activities without undue fatigue or physical stress. It is the direct result of lifestyle choices and our behaviours around sleep, diet, physical activity, hygiene and relaxation. Exercising our body so that will positively impact our overall wellbeing involves a routine of movement that will support the current state of our physical appearance, and improve the overall health of the functioning body. In learning to love the body, appreciating its level of high performance and capabilities, it is also important to value rest and to know when to nurture the body.

Recovery is just as important as the exercise and physical activity.

Putting structure and rituals and a regular routine into place helps us maintain and form healthy habits that will sustain and move us forward into optimum physical health and general wellbeing. Being realistic with our current state of health and the general condition of our body is vitally important, both for personal safety and setting oneself up for success. Finding the right starting place, types of exercise and relaxation activities, and being aware of our food intake helps us to get off on the right foot.

Accept that you are responsible for your own actions. Hold yourself to account on the proposed plan and weekly schedule; tune into your body daily and reflect and review whether your schedule worked or needs refinement. Listening to your body when you first wake up in the morning and adjusting what you have proposed for the day, is being adaptable to changing circumstances and how you feel about your body. The subtle feelings of your body will be vital in helping you to adjust your physical and relaxation routines, to ensure maximum outcomes for optimum results. If you can measure your performance of wellbeing daily and weekly - not just quantity but quality too - you can better track your overall performance.

Think about how you move your body on Country. Consider when that aligns to the rhythm of nature and its seasons - for example, winter is a time of rest and nurture and recovery - and between seasons, be aware of the subtle weather changes and its impact on your proposed routine.

Emotional Wellbeing

Emotional wellbeing is the ability to produce positive emotions, moods, thoughts and feelings, and to adapt when confronted with adversity and stressful situations. Emotional wellbeing allows you to focus on the positive, and to manage any negative emotions and feelings you have in a given situation.

Emotional health is influenced by environmental factors, relationships, physical health, self-awareness and stress. An emotionally healthy individual is not happy all the time. If you are not experiencing negative emotions, you may be repressing your emotions.

For emotional wellbeing, it is important to:

- be able to share your feelings with others, and talk with someone about your emotional concerns;
- say 'no' when you need to, without feeling guilty;
- aim to feel content most of the time;
- feel you have a strong support network in your life, people that care about you;
- be able to relax.

To look after your mental wellbeing, focus on:

- talking about your feelings with people who will listen when you feel troubled;
- keeping active; eat well;
- keeping in touch;
- asking for help;
- taking a break and doing something you're good at.

Conscious parenting that promotes emotional wellbeing in early years:

- offers opportunities for play and learning that acknowledge children's beliefs and cultural backgrounds;
- encourages playing games where children learn to take turns
- provides opportunities to make choices;
- offers opportunities for children to talk about their feelings.

Equanimity

I first came across this concept in greater detail when undertaking a course on the principles of mindfulness techniques and skills, taught and researched by a leading expert in the field, Dr Kristen Neff.

Equanimity is calmness and composure in a difficult situation. It is defined as being able to maintain your emotions, especially in a bad or negative situation. For example, you react calmly when you are given bad news about your health or your job. It is the quality of being calm and even-tempered and maintaining composure.

In Buddhism, equanimity (Pali: *upekkha*; Sanskrit: *upeksa*) is one of the four sublime attitudes. It is considered to be neither a thought nor an emotion, but the steady conscious realisation of reality's transience. It is the ground for wisdom and freedom, and the protector of compassion and love.

Physical activity and meditation are pathways to equanimity. To maintain equanimity:
- Remind yourself that equanimity is key and always prevails
- Breathe, recite an equanimity mantra, and walk away
- Visualise your vagus nerve, take a breath and let it go.

Facing a challenging external environment will test your ability to remain resilient and emotionally well. But if you have in place awareness of some helpful practices that you can schedule within your day, it will help with your emotional fitness to endure troubled waters that can be imposed upon you.

For emotional fitness:
- Get quality sleep
- Exercise
- Eat healthy food
- Practise self-care
- Create structure in your life
- Practise mindfulness
- Meditate
- Ground yourself.

Get Quality Sleep

Sleep deprivation can impact the way you perceive and respond to your surroundings. In fact, a lack of sleep can cause people to react negatively to things they would otherwise perceive as normal experiences.

A good night's sleep is one of the most important things you can do to reduce your emotional instability and reduce irritability. Most adults should aim for somewhere between seven and nine hours each night. If you have trouble falling or staying asleep, you can do some things to improve your sleep overall and help you get through your days with less emotional turmoil, such as:

- Staying on a regular sleeping routine
- Avoiding alcohol and caffeine before bed
- Making sure your room temperature is comfortable (and cool)
- Shutting off lights and electronics at least an hour before bedtime.

Preparing for sleep is just as important as preparing for the day in your morning. Winding down your energy systems operating within your body and ensuring your body aligns to the going down of the sun will ultimately lead to a better sleep.

Exercise

It's no secret that you will feel better physically and mentally when your body is active. Exercise doesn't just fight a host of physical health problems; it is also a great way to maintain a more stable emotional system.

- Start small, and don't overdo it. If you're highly motivated to start, you may push yourself too hard and risk injury.

- Gradually increasing the duration and/or difficulty of your workouts slowly over time.
- Experiment with different types of exercise. Try out a variety of exercises helping you determine which form you like the most, which will make you more likely to be consistent. You may find that you prefer exercise with someone in a team and group of friends or an activity by yourself.
- Include stress-reducing workouts in your routine. In addition to strength training and cardio, consider taking up calming forms of exercise, like yoga or something I have found helpful in men is yin-yoga and restorative yoga. These forms of exercise combine movement with controlled breathing, and they may help you combat the negative stress.

Eat Healthy Foods

Maintaining a healthy diet, improves your mood by ensuring you get the nutrients needed for good mental health. If you're not sure where to begin, consider working with a professional, health coach or nutrition expert to determine a plan that will work for you.

Negative emotions can lead to urges to eat unhealthy foods, binge eat or skip meals altogether. You may find yourself turning to comfort foods to help you handle stress or depression. Unfortunately, this can turn into a cycle, because poor eating also impacts mood.

Practise Self-Care

The best way to reduce our emotional ups and downs is to make a commitment to yourself and understand self-care practices. When we don't practice and hold boundaries to the space of self-care, we let ourself down eroding the self-love we need to live a fulfilled life. Today we have expectations, pressures and increasing demands that we have to manage every day. Self-care at work and home is vitally important and we should plan and structure this into our life.

This can include any activities that help you feel fulfilled and cared for such as spending time with friends and family, engaging in other interests that you find stimulating or fun, managing stress positively such as walks in nature, meditation, going to movies and as discussed previously having a healthy eating plan throughout your week and weekend. As refenced in previous chapters, it is the simple things in life such as drinking good quality water and local fruit and vegetables that brings support self-awareness so we get better with self-care.

The time you spend on a self-care program will pay off if you can improve your emotional well-being. Take time for yourself to relax, meditate, or what will bring you back to a reclaimed you. When you say yes to YOU the journey to discovery your inner awesomeness allows you to be present to the people that are in your life.

Healthy Structure

Structure in our life includes working practices, house cleaning routines, parenting and relationship routines allowing us a base or a core part of our life that we function effectively from. When we find ourself experiencing periods of emotional instability we are either growing and learning something new, doing something that isn't serving us, or our being isn't charged enough with a sense of wellness.

We are likely to feel these low feelings during our downtime, when you have no other activities planned, so by creating a structured routine could help you stay occupied and more emotionally stable so we are always in a state of healing, wellness and equipping ourself with emotional certainty and clarity. Western culture talks about Health and Wellness where as First Nations bring a life and journey of healing. We are always healing and going deeper into understanding ourselves. When we have good structure in our life around healing, wellness and health; when life throws a curve-ball at us, we are better equipped to adapt and keep moving forward in life.

Creating a consistent daily schedule lets you know what to expect, which may help you feel better prepared to meet each day and more secure overall. Following a routine can also ensure you set aside time to spend on other healthy activities, such as exercising and practising self-care.

Mindfulness

Mindfulness involves learning to become more aware and observant of yourself and your surroundings and encourages you to live in the present. Living mindfully means paying attention to the sights, sounds, and smells around you, as well as the sensations within you. You can practise mindfulness at any time during our day by purposefully tuning in.

Mindfulness is helpful for reducing anxiety and managing stress. If you find yourself reacting emotionally to something that happened in the past or something that may occur in the future, consider taking a mindfulness break. Multi-tasking throughout our day will take a toll on our wellbeing. Start taking note of the taste of your food when you eat, pay attention to the feeling of the water over your body when swimming in the salty-ocean, notice the temperature of your morning daily cup of tea and lean into feeling the stretch of your body before you exercise or during a yoga session.

I particularly enjoy being mindful in nature, the sounds of birds, feeling gum leaves, smell of gum trees and listening to the wind travel through the Casuarina trees. My daily dose of nature allows me to ground and feel connected to my best self, so I may live a mindful conscious life.

Meditation

While mindfulness is something that you can engage in at any time, meditation is a more structured practice. It's often done in a quiet place that's free from distractions, which allows you to focus on something specific, like your breath, a specific object, or a mantra. Scheduling regular meditation sessions for set time periods may help you manage any stress in your life.

Research on meditation suggests that the practice has a number of benefits, less anxiety, better over mood and increases your levels of awareness. Loving kindness meditation may increase feelings of self-acceptance and self-kindness while reducing the inner-critic that plays out in our mind every day.

Mindfulness meditation is a combination of both of these techniques. Mindfulness meditation is structured, meaning it involves setting aside a certain amount of time to allow yourself to get comfortable and focus. Generally, mindfulness meditation encourages you to pay attention to your body and breath, while noticing thoughts as they occur.

Grounding Yourself

Mindfulness is a key component of grounding. If there are times when you feel overwhelmed with emotion, techniques based on mindfulness can help you focus your attention. They work by pulling your thoughts away from the intense emotion, and directing your attention toward something more neutral, like a sight, smell, sound, or sensation.

One grounding technique, called the 5-4-3-2-1 method, relies on your senses to focus your attention on your surroundings. To try this method, focus on:

- Five things you see
- Four things you can touch
- Three things you hear
- Two things you smell
- One thing you taste.

Some other grounding techniques include:

- Engaging in a breathing exercise
- Snapping a rubber band gently on your wrist
- Holding an ice cube or running sand or soil through your hands
- Smelling eucalypt trees, salt in the air, burning candle or a cooking spice
- Touching something soft, like a towel or flower petal, and noting the texture
- Observing your surroundings and referencing the objects in the room or outside space and begin to notice the uniqueness of your space and place. Try and remember the key features and notice in subtle changes to the place

Emotional Wellness in the Workplace

Factors such as financial stability, workload, family, health and social interaction can all have an impact on your emotional wellbeing. If your emotional wellbeing is reduced, it's likely that your performance and effectiveness at work will suffer as a result.

We often find in work situations that a person who is performing well is given more work and rewarded with more challenging tasks for growth. It is often said that to get something done, give it to a busy person. But too often in work places, we see people who have a reputation of churning out high quality work burn out when they are loaded up with work.

Be aware of this possibility. It is important that everyone feels okay with communicating their boundaries and has good communication about their capacity and needs. This is bound up with self-esteem, and for building self-esteem everyone should learn to understand and pay attention to the Self-Esteem Triad in their interactions throughout the working day: boundaries, needs and emotion.

Working in your Business health trumps everything else, emotional wellness is the fundamental factor that contributes to performance in work teams. Patrick Lencioni in his book, - *The Advantage* describes for key disciplines. Build a Cohesive leadership team, create Clarity, overcommunicate clarity and Reinforce Clarity. *'The single greatest advantage any company can achieve is organization health.'*

Spiritual Wellbeing

> " Higher than dull matter are the senses, higher than the sense is the mind. Higher than the mind is the intelligence. Higher than the intelligence is the immortal self.
> **Bhagavad Gita 6.6**

Pay attention to your spiritual wellbeing. Hinduism teaches that 'to live with wisdom means to live in such a way that one's physical, emotional, and spiritual faculties are nourished and one's thoughts, words and deeds are attuned to the self within the body. When we forget we are something other than the physical body and mind, we suffer all the vulnerabilities inherent in that body and mind.' (*understandinghinduism.org*)

It may not be a popular word, but suffering is a universal experience. We all suffer physically and emotionally. But as we look to our spiritual wellbeing, we begin to develop a deeper self-awareness, and we learn to acknowledge suffering without identifying with it. Transformation begins when we use our intelligence to take control of the reins of what might be called the sixth sense, the mind.

Keeping It All Together as One

Understanding How Relationships Impact Our Wellbeing
All aspects of our wellbeing are influenced by the transmission of energy within ourself, and our interactions with the people that come into our life. A useful coaching model in navigating the self and ensuring we remain connected to our inner self is the *Self-Esteem Triad*, this model is discussed in Sharon Person book - '*Ultimate You Quest Edition*'. This model places the Self in the middle

of the triangle, bringing awareness to our Boundaries, Needs and Emotions. Those three factors shape and nurture aspects of our Self and the interactions we have with other people.

Keeping ourself all together can sometimes be a challenge when certain people come into our life and test our Boundaries, Needs and Emotions. If we stay true to our Self and use grounding techniques and routines to ensure the wellbeing elements stay in place, we will be able to maintain our levels of abundance and self-love necessary to live a rich and fulfilled life.

The Importance of Environment

Our environment influences us and makes us, so understanding how it impacts our wellbeing will assist us to navigate through our environment with greater harmony. Country, community or our home, shapes who we become. If we understand the environment - the uniqueness of trees, the home we live in, the rivers and community groups we invest ourself in - we begin to understand our roots. This especially includes our family, which most would agree shapes who we are and become.

Our culture, tribes, families, school, government and community are all parts of our environment and they have expectations, norms and standards that influence our behaviour. Sometimes these norms don't sit well with us and impact how we feel about our behaviour. Sometimes, too, the work we do impacts on our physical wellbeing.

If we understand nature and how it works, we can begin to align ourself with nature, just as we do with the seasons when we dress according to the weather the day presents to us. If a storm is approaching and the forecast informs us that a severe weather warning is approaching, we don't go and plan for a day at the beach, do we?

With this mindset, behavioural flexibility gives us our greatest strength as we move, work, live and play. Ultimately, movement of our body on Country, when aligned, makes us feel better and lifts our vibration.

Creating Consciousness in our Daily Life

When we begin to understand the value of being conscious in our daily life, it becomes important to maintain this level of awareness. When our vibration drops, perhaps due to lack of sleep or bad choices relating to food or drink, we notice that we are not feeling our best. They say there is no turning back when we choose an ascension towards the desired life we choose.

An early morning routine with sacred rituals is helpful in embracing daily life. To maintain consciousness and awareness of what is important to your inner self, spend some quality time each day writing, goal setting, journaling and practicing exercises for the mind, body and soul.

Sometimes our consciousness will slip back into the grind of life, the rigid structures that can tighten their grip on our soul and stop us from living the true life we desire and deserve. We are often un-aware that we perhaps slip back into old habits that don't serve our self and the people that matter most. If we are accountable only to our self and our higher purpose in life, we begin to hold these values and we become intrinsically motivated to always keep our level of consciousness.

The Art of Non-Attachment

Stewardship for a More Wholistic and Happy Life

Many conscious thought leaders, spiritual teachers, and in particular First Nation people, have always described and articulated the value in practising the art of detachment, walking on earth as custodians. When we recognise that we don't 'own' anything, we are able to live a life of caring, inspiring and enriching our experiences throughout our life. We are merely travelling on the Earth and one day we will depart, taking with us only memories, experiences, and the good deeds we have undertaken to inspire others to care for people and place.

The art of withdrawing the desire from the lesser things, letting them fall away, allows you to harness the power to reach the heights of what a human being can attain. Remember that you can't control others. When you separate yourself from others and respond instead of reacting, you can find your own happiness, and it allows you to flow more into life. The spiritual law of attachment is about trust and surrender rather than control.

> **"** When you are no longer tied to the outcome of how it must be, you free yourself up to abundant possibilities.
>
> **Kaiser**

Some people choose to recognise the value in asset wealth and income generation, and this is all good. We need to recognise, and have a healthy relationship with, our currency of trade on Country, which is money. We need money to live an epic and abundant life. But land, people and capital are the basis for real wealth. If we can choose a lifestyle that sustains and cares for land and people, and generates capital that will ensure they remain connected and in alignment for future generations, then we can truly say we are generating a conscious life-style, business and trade on Country that we can pass on for our next generation, our grandchildren.

Resilience

I have described and covered many resources, skills and frameworks that help us remain balanced and live a centred life. I feel that in enduring the challenges of life, we grow. To bounce back from life's challenges, we need a good capacity for resilience. This model is shared widely, and I use it regularly in working with my clients and in my own life.

Most definitions of resilience refer to the ability to bounce back from adversity and hardships. Whilst this is true, it can be misleading. Resilience is not something we are born with or without. It is an ongoing process which can be learned, practised and improved over time. These days, many of us can find ourselves prioritising immediate productivity over steady, long-term growth, which can lead to a plethora of undesirable outcomes such as burnout or complete disruption of work-life balance.

Sometimes our resilience will feel higher or lower than usual, but there are five key pillars which, when strengthened, will enable us to be resilient even in the toughest of situations. However, it is important to remember that resilience is a daily practice. By building it into our daily routine, we can enhance the good days and not just get through the bad.

Resilience is best described as bounce-back-ability. It is the ability to recover quickly from difficulties, adapt to life's adversities, and cope with the mundane stresses of everyday living. There are four types of resilience: physical resilience, mental resilience, emotional resilience and social resilience.

The Five Pillars of Resilience

Self-Awareness

It can seem as if the most resilient people have no trouble putting on a brave face and shutting out their emotions when required. But in reality, resilience comes from being able to accurately recognise, process and regulate our emotions. Sometimes, allowing ourselves to be vulnerable is the most resilient action possible. By working on our self-awareness, we can build the ability to react to external situations in sustainable and mindful ways.

Check in with yourself regularly and make time to consciously ask yourself how you're doing right now. We often live too much of our time stuck in the past or in anticipation for the future, but when it comes to building self-awareness, remaining present is a key factor. Whilst planning and hoping for the future can be extremely beneficial, it's all about balance, so remember to ask yourself how you are and nurture each moment as it comes.

Self-Care

Self-care looks different for everyone and can be practised in a huge range of ways. The concept of self-care has become more and more visible in the media, particularly during Covid lockdown. The increase in media coverage is certainly positive, but it can be easy to forget the true meaning and reasoning behind its importance. By recognising that sustainable self-care is vital to authentic resilience, we can break down the stigma that self-care is selfish. After all, you can't pour from an empty cup.

Positive Relationships

Humans are built to have connections with other people; we are not wired to take on the world alone. Good levels of resilience has a lot to do with building and nurturing healthy and supportive relationships with friends, family and professional networks and being ok leaning into other people. Positive relationships do not mean an absence of disagreement, but trusting others to be there for you when life may throw you an imperfect wave that you stumble on an aspect of your life. Mutual respect and reciprocated effort come with the territory of being a good friend, family member or co-worker, and by working on our relationships we can remain connected and supported.

Purpose

Our purpose helps to shape our mindset and attitude towards others and the events that we experience in our day-to-day lives. There are many different places that we can harness that sense of purpose from, such as our faith, loved ones, culture, responsibilities, philosophical beliefs, and the list goes on infinitely. Whilst being purpose-driven won't instantly increase your resilience, it will gradually enhance your strength and energy when it comes to dealing with the ups and downs life can throw at you. Finding meaning and learning in our experiences is the best way to push forward and live resiliently.

Mindfulness

Mindfulness is a state of open awareness towards something you may be doing, enjoying eating some fruit and experiencing all the senses so as to enrich our inner world. When we observe our thoughts and feelings, we open up all the richness of life and awakening to the experience.

Yin Yoga and The Duality Concept

Where China Meets India and Yoga Meets the Chinese Feminine
In the final chapter I will talk about a pledge, the concept of 'pause for a cause', and how we can bring wellness back onto Country. Life has evolved to become fast, complicated and very much in the patriarchal system. To collectively build consciousness, we need to and embrace more *yin*, less *yang*; we must become more matriarchal, have more gratitude, encourage more softness in our men, and in our women. More simplicity, calmness and clarity will bring us more certainty. Then we may see ourselves, and that leads to greater awareness of identity of self and our Country.

Yin yoga is a beautiful blend of Chinese and Indian philosophy in which the body is seen as embraced by the movement of energy across its energy centres. This is much like the way songlines and energy move across planet earth as collective energy, and the natural flow of energy from west to east as planet earth moves in this direction. All events and experiences on earth are a reflection of energy. The way to cultivate more balance is to recognise that our system, people and structures today do not serve the people or the planet.

Let us embrace a bit of slowness, and recognise the need to nurture some sacred balance as a collective community. An event that cultivates a collective and shared consciousness shows a responsible community that values people, their unique self, and how we all belong to one another. All living things depend on us acting more responsibly. I call Australia 'to act its age' and be more responsible in caring for people and place. Let us demonstrate this to the rest of the world. Let us cultivate collective gratitude.

Dr David Sinclair is a leading world authority on genetics and longevity. In his new book *Lifespan,* he reveals a bold new theory for why we age. He writes that aging 'is a disease, and that disease is treatable'. The insights include how we can slow down, or even reverse aging. The book describes how through genetic programming in the near future, we may not just be able to feel younger, but actually become younger. For the health of ourselves and planet, we all need to slow down. Lifestyle changes, such as intermittent fasting, cold exposure, exercising with the right intensity, and eating less meat have been shown to help us live younger and be healthier for longer.

Embracing simplicity, calmness and slow moments in our life, and embracing a healthy lifestyle habit, will be good for everyone, and we might just slip into world peace!

Chapter Ten

A Pledge for Collective Gratitude on Country

To Cultivate Collective Consciousness.
9 August - United Nations – Custodianship

> **"** Ancient mystics knew that intention is the key to life and how life unfolds. It works not only on a personal level, but also trans-personally. Intention can affect the collective and eventually create changes, for better or worse.
>
> **Shakti Durga, www.shaktidurga.com**

L et's say you have an example of personal change in mind. You decide to move from a mindset of 'I'm not good enough' to one of 'I am good enough'. If you make that kind of shift, and do your inner work around it, the difference in the way people will treat you will be absolutely astonishing. You will see it in all of relationships. You will see the many positive changes that come once you start to believe in yourself, and you start to do the work of intending there to be love and peace.

Take a look at the collective level. Consider the stock markets, for example. Generally, they go up and down. You may wonder how they can be so volatile sometimes. There are certain technical reasons to do with how people trade, but there's also the collective consciousness. People lose confidence in a market. It catches like a virus, and then no-one believes it's going to be any good. The whole thing crashes. Similarly, when everybody is thinking positively, the market goes up and up.

There are forces at work not only in us, but between us. There is a matrix of thought that exists in any culture, that tells us what's correct and what's not correct. We end up trying to align our lives with what the matrix will say. For example, one example of mass consciousness agreements might be that it's okay for women or men to get married at 15 years of age. Reality then matches the ideas that lie within laws, but also applies to things that are more subtle, such as how we feel about things and the kinds of value judgments we hold. These subtle factors all change the way things are.

What happens when you get 25 million people focused on a problem? What is the effect going to be? It's going to energise and grow the problem through the power of intention. If we can collectively utilise visioning techniques, things might turn around and more positive changes fall into place. At our current level of consciousness, we don't know the answers to the challenges facing the natural world. We definitely know we've got to clean the place up. We've got to have people loving the land and loving each other - empowering people and place. It seems clear that our inner attitude and what we're visioning for the future will affect what happens.

In *The Power of Eight*, Lynne McTaggart sets out the power of intention. Essentially, before something happens, there's a certain probability that it will happen, but it has not yet solidified into something happening until it happens. When the jelly sets, so to speak, is when it actually happens. It's quantum physics 101. McTaggart explains how science is now saying the most essential ingredient in creating our universe is the consciousness that observes it. It is a joint effort between the observer and the observed, and what we focus on tends to grow. In Coaching we say 'what we focus on is what we get' as Paul Kelly's song 'Be careful what you pray for' ...we just might get it.

This implies that observation and visioning, the key involvement of consciousness, get the coagulated energy jelly to actually set in a certain pattern, which creates a certain reality. If actually looking at and observing something is changing it, what if you actually have a clear intention when you go into it? What does that do? This approach spawned a whole range of intentional experiments.

Several of the central figures in quantum physics argue that the universe is democratic and participatory. At a research laboratory at Princeton University, scientists created a sophisticated scholarly research program grounded in hard science. Over 25 years, scientists Jahn and Dunne led what became a massive international effort to quantify what is referred to as micro-psychokinesis, which means the ability to make things happen, the effect of the mind on random event generators. A random event generator performs the electronic 21st century equivalent of tossing a coin, to see whether heads or tails lands upwards. The output of these machines, the computerised equivalent of heads or tails, was controlled by random alternation frequency of positive and negative pulses. At a university in Texas, they demonstrated that human thoughts can affect the direction in which fish swim; also, the movement of other animals like gerbils and mice, and the breakdown of cells in the laboratory. Another study involves attempts to influence the throw of a dice. They have shown that human thought influences physical matter.

These are such important scientific studies. One of the things that happens in life is that we're faced with problems. The problem might be that I'm not getting respect in my relationships, or a fire is out of control in my country. In the physical dimensions, the problem has already happened, so the first priority is: *How do I make myself safe and how do I survive?* That's the most important thing. Then after that, the question becomes: *How do I turn it around?* To turn it around, we're actually using the dimension of our mind. The mind is able to visualise a future and turn the ship; we are able to visualise a future and see where we are heading. If we did this in our relationships, imagine what would happen if we reached an empowered group of people, and they consistently visualised Australia as a lush and fertile country with good rainfall and healthy communities.

When the Aboriginal Australians managed the land, it was described by Bill Gammage as the 'Greatest Estate on Earth'. Bruce Pascoe provides some beautiful insights into how Australia was managed, and describes what the settlers and Government officials observed and saw across Country. They saw crops growing and houses and grain storage, and cachets of tools located in strategic places around Country. There was crop rotation and they did it seasonally, and they did it with great respect for the land. The people never over-burdened the land. Places that are now desert were very fertile when the land was understood, worked with love, and the people recognised their role as stewards, custodians.

What would happen if we collectively held a vision for that?

Investigators who study prayer have found that it works better specifically than it does generally. In other words, praying for a specific person can have positive impact on that person. So, pray for and target your vision of protection on anyone you know who is in the path of a disaster like a fire. Your love and your vision will help protect them.

Let's start holding a collective vision of a country that is not polluted. Where people value trees; they like trees, and want to plant trees, and they don't want to pollute. The basic stuff. If we all did that, I think we could create a vision for the future that would be very different from the Doomsday prophecy that is alive within some of our culture.

I believe the new day is coming. But it takes a lot of strength to be able to keep your mind on a positive vision when disasters are unfolding. Let us work collectively to create a vision that holds the right values for people to belong in a clean and green place that is loving and caring, a vision that has values that nurture self-relationships and caring for Country for everyone. This is the vision and future we should all hold onto for the benefit our children's children. We don't own Country, Country owns us. We are all stewards of the Earth but we must respect and earn this title as a custodian.

We are now witnessing the realisation within our economy that the environment is critical for success in all aspects of our society. Business is taking up the challenge with the recognition that we truly live in a closed looped system. The circular economy is fundamental to dealing with waste and the pollution of our homes. It begins with how we live and the lifestyle we choose to embrace. We all need to do our part.

The journey to self, and how we value personal development as we live with each other, will strengthen our relationships across our communities and in business. But we must do everything in our power to reach out and empower others not to be left behind. We need our First Nations people. They have been hit by a bomb since white settlers arrived on this country. We have imposed on them the western culture of drinking, and eating sugar, which were foreign to them. The Australian Aborigines lived in a utopia – their Dreamtime, but they have survived.

The 9th of August is International Day of the World's Indigenous Peoples. I am making a pledge to signal to the world that we must pause for a global cause, as I have highlighted in this book. We must send a signal of respect from western culture, that we are listening to First Nation peoples and that we value their wisdom and knowledge of how-to live-in harmony with nature. Australia is home to the oldest surviving culture on Earth. Let us honour this with a National Day of Pause, in which we show respect, gratitude and love for Country. We can all move forward together as a group, when we pay respect to the simple things in life. Let us embrace simplicity and value the slow lane in life.

Australia is built on traditional ceremony which pays respect and connects people to Country. I have witnessed many such ceremonies. Let us bring ceremony back on Country for all cultures. We pay lip service with cultural activities for a week during Reconciliation and NAIDOC, but to truly recognise the ancient land we live on, let us honour this wisdom so it can take us to a new day.

Western culture is disconnected from the true essence of life and the power of nature. They try their best to control everything in their attempt to succeed and dominate, when really it would be better to just sit still, become humble and listen to those beings who are so much wiser...

My people are not threatened by silence. They are completely home in it. They have lived for thousands of years with Nature's quietness. My people today, recognise and experience in this quietness, the great Life-Giving Spirit, the Father of us all. It is easy for me to experience God's presence. When I am out hunting, when I am in the bush, among the trees, on a hill or by a billabong;

these are the times when I can simply be in God's presence. My people have been so aware of Nature. It is natural that we will feel close to the Creator.

From Dadirri – Inner Deep Listening and Quiet Still Awareness, Miriam Rose Ungunmerr Baumann, Senior Australian of the Year 2020

We honour the ANZACS at the sunrise, marking our respect to those that fought for freedom. As the sun goes down, let us do this for Country. Let us have a day of Caring for Country. Let it not be a day of celebration and boozing, but a day of planting trees and ceremony, to create a new future, a vision for a new Earth. Many cultures, one Earth. I invite the participation all the cultures from different parts of the world that call Australia home.

I have seen many of my First Nations brothers and sisters fight for culture with anger and frustration for too long, to the detriment of their health. It breaks my heart today to see too many cultural warriors die too early. Poor health choices, you say, but I see genocide and human rights violations on this Country. Sorry Day is a start, but for Australia to truly recognise the ancient nomads that survived climate change, we need their culture and vibration on Country (song) to once again be alive and thriving.

Paul Kelly said that from small things big things grow. I ask you that the 9th of August, the day the world recognises as International Day of the World's Indigenous Peoples, is a day of collective gratitude. I call on all Australians to pause and pay respect to Country. My vision is for a public holiday. My vision is for communities across Australia to embrace the values of wellness on Country on this day, with ceremony led by our First Nations people. May we finally acknowledge that we do not own a piece of dirt on this Country, and let us start by embracing the concept of stewardship, as custodians of Country.

Uncle Steve Goldsmith once said to me, 'It is not reconciliation we need but conciliation. this country belongs to all of us. We, us black fellas, have always welcomed new people around our camp fire.'

The Afghan cameleers, the Irish, Scottish and many other immigrants have married and interbred with First Nations people, but let us not forget the traditional ceremony of ancient ancestors of this land and its Dreaming stories.

" It is common for Australians to look elsewhere for spiritual enlightenment. we climb the steps of ancient temples, pray in churches throughout Europe, but we have rarely chosen to examine the spirituality and philosophy of the world's oldest and most sustainable culture here. Australia.
From *Country* by Bill Gammage and Bruce Pascoe

Lessons from a Tree in an Ancient Land

Australia and its people have endured hardship. First Nations people have survived, and continue to survive. Boat people, new arrivals, have their own story of hardship. The land is harsh, as mother Nature is harsh, yet soft and nurturing. When I reflect on the great deserts that lie in the heart of this large continent, I remind myself of the distance travelled by the westerly winds that have passed through the ancient land. And I immediately think of a barren tree standing in the ground, providing shade for the few that will pass this track across the central desert plains of Australia.

Lessons from a tree come to many who travel across our land in the hot, baking sun. Divine love is accessible to those who are 'humbler than a blade of grass, more tolerant than a tree, and ready to offer all respect to others while expecting none in return' (Chaitanya

Mahaprabhu). By cultivating these qualities, the heart becomes a fertile field where the flower of divine love can blossom. The Bhakti Yoga path describes the tree analogy and how the tree tolerates inconveniences for the welfare of others. Trees stand directly under the burning summer sun even as they provide shade for those similarly afflicted. In the winter they provide warmth as we stoke a fire around a campfire or load up the wood heater. In the dry season, a mango tree provides its juicy fruit to sweetly reward our thirst. The constant presence of our eucalypt gum tree provides all-round scent that brings us back to a common place: Australia.

Smell is the last sense that departs our soul when we pass this life. The smell of eucalypt is iconic to any Australian heart. When a tree is cut down, it sacrifices its body without protest, providing timber for building and wood for heating. In this sense, trees truly symbolise service to others.

" Blessed are those who plant trees under
whose shade they will never sit.
Indian proverb

Growth In Stillness

Take time for stillness to listen to self, self is nature in progress.

> Even if your plans have changed, even if your timeline is different, even if this year has not unfolded the way you thought it would - you are not falling behind. ... real growth is not always just constant forward motion. ... Growth is letting yourself settle, it's letting yourself blossom, it's letting yourself see how much good is already in your life before you hunger for more.
>
> You are allowed to take days to grieve, to do nothing. You are allowed to press your plans back until they make more sense. You do not exist on a single schedule; your fate is not to arrive at each set point at precisely the second you think you should. That's not what you're here for. That's not what this whole thing is about.
>
> You cannot miss the exit.
>
> There are no wrong turns.
>
> Life is a living, breathing thing - because it's an extension of you. ... We are not only making progress when we are clearly, discernibly growing. We are also making progress when we take time to simply be.
>
> **From *This Is Your Evergreen Reminder That Slowing Down Is Not Falling Behind* by Brianna Wiest**

When we see country differently, we see more of her wonder and treat her like a park instead of scrub. Aboriginal people didn't see the land as scrub or wilderness; they saw Country as their home, all of it. The formation of a treaty between Aboriginal and Torres Strait Islander people and non-Indigenous Australians, I believe, will make us a more whole country and bring to the fore an ancient culture that understands that Country is our home.

Most Australians know that, rather than pursuing a more attractive lifestyle, the more sustainable way is to adopt a more modest lifestyle and behaviour that supports the wellbeing of people and planet. We are beginning to see changes, but we cannot allow our country to be led by idealogues towards self-interest and disregard for the Earth. If they want riches at the expense of the planet, we cannot allow it. We need to examine how we trade on Country. Does it serve the future generations, our children's children?

When we see the world in a different way, it will influence how we spend our money. Why are people trying so hard to escape their lives? Why do they despair of the world we have created? If we ask why people are choosing to flee from it, we need to look at the values that underpin this choice. Perhaps these values do support our home, Mother Earth, but our lifestyle does not. Capitalism believes in profit. Many business people see a tree or body of water and see a potential sale in this product. This attitude to the national estate robs the majority of people and rewards the selfish individual. The system of capital exploitation has created a world of comfort and advances in medicine and food technology, but the impacts still include poverty, drug use and environmental destruction.

Compassion

Karuna: (Hindi) active, intelligent and directed compassion

The 9th of August should also be about compassion and gratitude. As we try to appreciate a broader perspective of a compassionate lifestyle, we cannot help but feel concerned about how we treat the Earth, considered to be one of our mothers by so many as we awaken. The great mother. How we treat Mother Earth affects the wellbeing of everyone. The Earth is being stripped of its resources and waste is still be created at a rate that outstrips what Mother Earth can provide to sustain people.

You might ask: *How does compassion, kindness and building a culture of cleansing and opening our hearts deal with the destruction of our homes? Karuna* is a Sanskrit word that means compassion, which itself literally means to 'feel with others'. When we act on compassion, *karuna* is active, intelligent and directed, showing concern for the suffering of others and our home. If we love our home as much as the people in our lives, our community, our neighbours and family, this is thoughtful and committed action. The Earth is our mother, and she sustains us, keeps us alive.

To practise *karuna* towards the Earth requires that we think about the problem, diagnose it, and see how we can help. Looking at our problems with a deeper perspective requires deeper compassion and self-love, consideration of how we might choose to live with more compassion. The root cause of environmental pollution is pollution within the ecology of the human heart. Even if we manage to clean the air, rivers and oceans, people will pollute them again unless we reform their internal ecology. A toxic greed has contaminated people's minds. Greed is an obsession, an addiction. It can never be satisfied; the more you get, the more you want. Greed hardens the heart and allows us to rationalise cruelty and justify crime. Greed inspires envy, divides families, provokes wars and blinds us to our real self-interest.

The Bhagavad Gita calls greed a symptom of ignorance, which covers the natural virtues of the soul. So, when we have a practice of meditation and rituals that nurture our self, fulfil our true purpose and cultivate self-love, we are inspiring others to purify the inner ecology and connect our heart and mind into a whole, centred, loving being.

It's our service to live in balance with the Earth, seeing the larger picture, recognising the effects of our actions and exercising moderation. We are witnessing the consequences of the depletion of resources, climate change and a dirty world. We are seeing changes from government and big business, but we need to sustain this momentum and ensure our communities remain the focal point. American and Professor *David* Orr in his book - *Ecological Literacy: Educating our children for a sustainable World* writes about how we bring language that encourages to love, see and feel into our landscapes. Ecological literacy allows the mind to be curious about mother nature. *David Orr's* work reminds me of many conversations I have had with First Nation elders, when you understand our language, you understand our culture and connection to county.

As Mahatma Gandhi said: 'Be the change you wish to see in the world.' If we inspire people to see the Earth as a sacred creation, they will have access to a uniquely powerful tool of inner and outer transformation.

The pace of advancements in technology and innovation we are witnessing is inspiring. It can assist with how we trade on Country and planet Earth, and the benefits will assist people to live more in harmony with their communities. But for the sake of our future, it is imperative that we take a step back to reflect on where we're going and what's happening to our quality of life. We are so tuned into computer screens, social media and an auditory-digital world, that we see many people no longer experiencing the joy of watching a sunset or hearing birdsong as the sun goes down. How long can we keep up this hectic pace of technological advancement? We have good intentions with technology and advancements in science, but they should not come at the expense of our overall wellbeing.

Today we are seeing people wanting to live green; they want to play a role in positive change. Recognise that you are nourished and sustained by nature. Feel yourself part of the whole. You have a relationship with everything and everyone. A personal commitment to the health of the environment matures when we learn to be kind to all beings, from other people to animals, trees, fish and our oceans. Most importantly, to cultivate this commitment to the health of our system, we must be kind to ourself. To explore ways to cultivate kindness and interconnectedness with the natural world is to explore ways to consume less.

In most parts of Australia, August sits well in terms of our weather systems. August is a time between seasons, an opportunity to reflect before the year draws to a close, with the festive season of party and celebration. In August, let us begin to experience gratitude for what Country is producing, aligning to business, society and our soils.

August aligns to some significant events in land rights, as in Paul Kelly's song *From Little Things Big Things Grow* and the Wave Hill Walk-Off story, but I feel that to bring this date into alignment with the politics of this Country misses the point. Coming from a true heart and the call for truth that is being asked of us, let us recognise this and place our best foot forward, showing ourselves and the rest of the world what our country is to its full potential. We have an opportunity to demonstrate to the world who we truly are and to be genuine about our identity, by seeing, observing, listening and being consciously aware of who we are as a nation. When we see a child born into this world, we see a playful, adventurous soul who has been born free, seeking to learn and absorb all that the child is experiencing. Mother Earth allows us to roam free and experience the joy of life.

Let us act our true age and be mature about the topic of birth and our home, the oldest land continent of the Earth with the oldest surviving culture on Earth. Acting our age means being adults, and being honest with ourselves and as a nation. This land has its own sovereign identity.

We are reborn every morning as we wake to seek new beginnings, fresh from our experiences the day before and recharged, rested and ready to seek new experiences as we journey through this place called life. Our Mother Earth and all her living creatures are reborn from every rotation and within our 24-hour cycle.

United Nations

In 1992, Dr M Yunupingu, Aboriginal educator, musician and ambassador, was appointed Australian of the Year. Dr Yunupingu was born in Arnhem Land and began teaching at the Yirrkala School in his early twenties. He gained a Bachelor of Education in 1987 and subsequently became the first Indigenous Australian to be appointed a school principal. Dr Yunupingu developed a progressive curriculum that incorporated both western and Aboriginal knowledge traditions. In 1986 he founded the acclaimed Australian band Yothu Yindi, which blended Aboriginal music with western rock music.
*Source: **Australian commonwealth government.***

Yothu Yindi wrote the hit song *Treaty* to highlight the Hawke Government's broken promise of a treaty with Aboriginal people.

> **"** I heard it on the radio, I saw it on the television.
> *Treaty* **by Yothu Yindi**

In 1992, Yothu Yindi performed the song in New York to help launch the United Nations International Year of the World's Indigenous Peoples. Yothu Yindi travel was funded by the Federal Government, by the Australian Prime Minister Paul Keating. Dr M Yunupingu was named Australian of the Year for his role in 'building bridges of understanding between Aboriginal and non-Aboriginal people'. He was the second member of his family to receive the honour, after his brother Galarrwuy in 1978.

The 9th of August is not attached to any political party, but to all cultural groups. If we connect with Country, we seem to have more harmony in our lives. The last time I saw Uncle Steve Goldsmith was out the front of the South Australia Migration Museum. I have a flood of emotions at my vivid memory of talking with him about 'lore and food on Country for everyone'. A wonderful man.

Australia has the oldest surviving literature in the songlines that travel across the globe. This movement of energy across our landscape is important for the rest of the world, so we can keep a balance of the masculine and feminine energies between our families, communities and our relationships.

It's a fact that most countries don't celebrate the day they were invaded by colonial settlers. If one person isn't standing in his or her truth, this holds us all back. We have unpacked this in previous chapters within the topic of equality. We are all in this sinking boat together, are we not? Cultural truth and our own personal story are the personal brands we hold.

No-one can take away your true story. First Nations people today say they have survived. They did indeed survive, because they dug in deep and did not shy away from the truth. But it cost many early Aboriginal activists a short life when no-one was listening or even awake. To be seen, heard and validated is the greatest gift of love we can give to someone or a collective group of people. It is immensely healing.

I reflect on the many Aboriginal brothers and sisters who stood in their truth and are no longer with us because not once did they hide behind a false self. They died because of the emotional trauma and a fight that they dared not back away from. The strength and good of standing in self-power and owning truth is powerful and transformational, not only for oneself, but for others whom we inspire to take their own journey of truth. To stand strong in our story, our personal story, is the brand and integrity that we trade on Country. Nelson Mandela endured one of the greatest fights of his life by standing for what was right. Ghandi took his truth into the streets of India and stood, peaceful, in his truth for the betterment of his people.

At this stage of evolution, as we stand at the crossroads and countries around the world protest, can we be clear about what is truly occurring within our consciousness as people awaken to the truth? Michael Jackson said, 'I'm a lover not a fighter.' I believe we need men to be both, and to do this well. For what is true, to fight is to love.

Wellness on Country isn't owned by the Trade Practices Act. It is owned by the collective individuals who own their truth in self, the truth of who they are. South Australia, my home State, has embraced social truth and what is right. A truly great South Australian was Dame Roma Mitchell. She was an Australian lawyer, Judge and State Governor, the first woman to hold a number of notable positions in Australia. She was the first woman judge, and the first woman to be a Queen's Counsel, Chancellor of an Australian university, and the Governor of an Australian State. In 1981 she became the founding Chairwoman of the Australian Human Rights Commission. Mitchell worked for the rights of women, Aboriginals and the disabled.

Will Australia act its age and stand in its truth? This will hurt. If we see the land and Country for what it is, it will hurt to realise the pain that we all carry.

Early Truth - Eddy Mabo

Edward Koiki Mabo (June 1936-1992) was an Indigenous Australian man from the Torres Strait Islands known for his role in campaigning for Indigenous land rights in Australia, in particular the landmark decision of the High Court of Australia that overturned the legal doctrine of terra nullius ('nobody's land') that had previously characterised Australian law with regard to land and title. High court judges found in favour of Mabo, which led to the Native Title Act 1993 and established native title in Australia, officially recognising the rights of Aboriginal and Torres Strait Islander people in Australia to own and use the land on which their families had lived for millennia.

In 1981 at land rights conference at James Cook University, Mabo gave a speech in which he explained the land inheritance system on Murray Island. The significance of this in terms of Australian common law doctrine was noted by one of the attendees, a lawyer, who suggested there should be a test case to claim land rights through the court system. Perth-based solicitor Greg McIntyre was at the conference and agreed to take the case; he then recruited barristers Ron Castan and Bryan Keon-Cohen. McIntyre represented Mabo during the hearings.

Of the eventual outcome of that decision a decade later, Reynolds said it was a ten-year battle and it was a remarkable saga.

On 21 January 1992, Eddie Mabo died of cancer at the age of 55.

Five months later, on 3 June 1992, the High Court announced its historic decision to overturn the legal doctrine of terra nullius, which defined land which was supposedly 'uninhabited' as liable for government seizure. That decision ... is recognised for its landmark status.

Three years after Mabo died (the traditional mourning period for the people of Murray Island), a memorial service was held in Townsville. The next day, Mabo's gravesite was attacked by vandals who spray-painted swastikas and the word 'Abo' ... on his tombstone and removed a bronze bas-relief portrait of him. His family decided to have his body reburied on Murray Island. On the night of his reinternment, the Islanders performed their traditional ceremony for the burial of a Meriam king, a ritual not seen on the island for 80 years.

Wikipedia

Sense of Place - Cultivating Wellness Far and Wide

Our identity is shaped but our reflection of self is not. When we pause and look at ourselves, who we are becoming, we see only aspects of ourselves and the joy of growing into a better person. I say to Australia: let us act our age. I see aspects of our society that are immature and not aspects of an adult.

Part of the responsibility of adulthood, in my view, is to not always to take the celebration approach to our national public holidays, and embrace the booze culture for which we seem to be known across the world. If we were to act our age with regard to the oldest surviving culture on Earth, we would truly embrace the philosophy of custodianship that our First Nations people have always understood. It is time for Australia to lead by example to the rest of the world. We don't need to look up to America, Europe or Asia. We have our own self-worth, as a country worthy of our own love for the country we have been granted.

Collective Gratitude

This is a call to all Australians to embrace their own identify, to take the journey to be the best they can be and bring the concept of 'love on Country' to your own communities.

On the 9th of August I call for you to plant the seed, to draw the line in the sand and say to yourself, your community and our Country that you value, that you have gratitude for it and will care for people and place. This clearly sends a message to the rest of the world that we are 'born free' every day, free to choose the future we desire for our children's children and future generations, as custodians and stewards of our home, Mother Earth.

In the final stages of writing this book, I was fortunate to share the concept of a collective day of gratitude with Peter Goers on ABC Radio 891, whilst on my way home from a holiday. I had been visiting family and enjoying one of my favourite leisure activities, surfing the Pacific salt water on the east coast of Australia, as I have done for many years. As Peter famously says 'travel well' to all people he talks to, I did indeed 'travel well'.

This concept of moving across our home into the 'doing' of who we wish to be, the concept of 'Live – Well', is why I chose Living WELL as my business name. The great nomads, our first Australians, moved seasonally across Country, respecting what Country has to teach us, and always finding the time to find stillness before moving. They understood the importance of the doing and the being, or the task and relationship duality, for finding better ways to have the things we need, so we may give to others and inspire others to come on this journey.

When we are content within our home, our castle, we travel or move into the 'doing' with more wisdom and awareness. We trade on Country and do business that aligns with true purpose, that always recognises the key principles of caring for people and place, particularly so we have a culture that nurtures children's wellbeing, and at its core requires us to occasionally pause.

The *yin*, slowing down, and the matriarch bring back the sacred balance and encourage us to build collective consciousness amongst communities, founded on the concept of collective gratitude. The great slowing down means living a more modest lifestyle, so humans continue to live in harmony with each other and Country (nature). It means to not compare ourselves to those in the northern hemisphere, but to embrace indigenous wisdom, acknowledge our mistakes to First Nations people, and encourage our communities to embrace simplicity, slowness and gratitude on Country.

This book has been about men embracing the feminine as much as it has been about how we trade better on Country. It has been a plea for us to truly act our age and stand up to our true identity. This country has the oldest surviving culture, land and people on Earth. We need to start acting as if we own this story. We have many cultures in Australia and we continue to be proud of the cultural diversity. But we need to pause and take a good look at ourselves and what we model to the rest of the world, so that we can find peace in our society. The world is looking for leadership and a focus on best practice in how we can live more in harmony. Today as I finish this book, we once again see the patriarchal system play out, with tensions and war breaking out in Eastern Europe. It is unnecessary, but as the Earth adjusts to a heightened frequency, we all have a role to play in bringing people back to the natural frequency we so desperately need - the sacred balance.

When we embrace more 'ecological literacy' into our culture, much like my home city of Adelaide where we see government, community, and schools embracing Kaurna language back onto 'place' we begin to see changes how people see country. As David

Orr, Professor of environmental studies at the pioneering liberal arts institution of Oberlin College in Ohio, writes insightfully and passionately about ecological literacy. He states that capable ecological literacy 'requires the more demanding capacity to observe nature with insight, a merger of landscape and mindscape.'

Uncle Lewis Yerloburka O'Brien reminds me of the Kaurna word for *mind* - *MukaMuka* meaning two ovals in that our mind works like a mirror concept our mind is a reflection of what we see in our environment.

> **"** You cannot get through a single day without having an impact on the world around you. What you do makes a difference, and you have to decide what kind of difference you want to make.
> **Jane Goodall**

Acknowlededgments

I am most grateful for 21 years of community service within the field of Local Government. This period of employment, I was most fortunate to work across a diverse range of sectors. Managing a diverse range of projects contributed to a broad understanding of community and government services. I formed wonderful friendships working for three Councils (Marion, Claire-Gilbert Valley and Onkaparinga). I particularly would like to acknowledge Mr Mark Searle, former CEO of the City of Marion and former Mayor Felicity Ann-Lewis at the time forged and demonstrated excellent leadership during a time when we accomplished some significant projects for the community, and I was honoured to have served under their leadership. Notably securing the funding for the (FINA) State Aquatic Centre and building strong relationships between Living Kaurna Culture Centre/Community and City of Marion.

Uncle Lewis O'Brien mentor, 92-year-old Kaurna elder of the Adelaide Plains and for our enjoyable Garfish lunches at the Carlisle Tavern in Ethelton down in the Port of Adelaide and for his time in the final parts of my writings always full of wisdom and insights bringing the two worlds into one.

To my friend Brett Aylen from '3 Wild Architects.com' for some of his insights into home design and industry issues within Australia and overseas.

Shakti Durga and Shanti Mission School for the Soul, on the east Coat of Australia and her community in Coorangbong and Morisett when I first discovered Kirtan and Bhakti yoga and my first trip to India with her spiritual community. Discovering yoga and sacred music at the time saved my emotional wellbeing. I will always be grateful.

The Coaching Institute and the founder Remi (Sharon) Pearson and finding a tribe of people that care and encourage each other to re-define and find deeper levels of love within self to share our story to inspire others to do the same.

My spirit brother's son Paul Dixon junior and our recent travels across southern Kaurna country and to all Kaurna country men Allan Sumner, Jamie Goldsmith, Karl Telfer and your Mums devotion to authentic story on country, Jack Buckskin, Jason Brodie, Max Mansell, Adrien O'Brien, Jeffery Newchurch, and Uncle Steve Goldsmith like so many aboriginal people passed away far too young. To Frank Wanganeen and Darren Wanganeen. To the Auntie's and their wisdom and looking out for this 'white fella' your spirit always looking out for me, thank you.

To the many people I have met working in remote parts of country, outback and who have devoted their life to serving in some of the most incredible places you can imagine. Let us not say the old metaphors of 'the harsh brutal outback' but re-label how we see country to enrich and see the beauty all that it is. So, this may inspire city folk to venture across this great land and bring back the goodness so we see remote country as beautiful and full of goodness.

My Surf community, in particular as a Life member of Port Noarlunga Surf Lifesaving Club (Tainbarilla) for keeping me grounded and reminding me 'Coops' and to all my surf Coaches which took me into coaching in the early days and seeing young nippers enjoying the salty sea.

My children Logan and Maggie may you continue to follow your dreams and always know my love for you both and the journey home.

Mum and Dad who have passed away but grateful for the sacrifice you made for my brother (my best mate) leaving a loving family behind and choosing a lifestyle of beach and bush.

The East Coast of Australia, and my endless trips of 'salt water healing' taking my 'desert dreaming' with me. The final stages of the manuscript' I enjoyed a final rest and review in a coastal community town taking the advice of Cal Newport's book 'Deep Rest' and found a little cabin nurturing myself to go through parts of my book and some reflections on life.

To country grateful for the path that I have travelled and for country teaching me the way how to live on country with heart. The deep contentment of the west wind travelling through the ancient Casuarina tree when we listen deep to the message that it has for us, then and only then do we move forward. It is to be ok with silence and sit on country.

In the language of the Yolngu people.

'yo manymak.'

Final acknowledgement to 'Old Man' and 'Amma Shanti'.